TRANSITIONS

Making Sense
of Life's Changes

William Bridges, Ph.D.

ADDISON-WESLEY PUBLISHING COMPANY
Reading, Massachusetts
Menlo Park, California • London • Amsterdam
Don Mills, Ontario • Sydney

Library of Congress Cataloging in Publication Data

Bridges, William, 1933–
  Transitions.

  Includes index.
  1. Life cycle, Human—Psychological aspects.
  2. Maturation (Psychology) 3. Social change.
  4. Social adjustment. 5. Adjustment (Psychology)
  I. Title.
  HQ799.97.U5B74   303.4   80-20044

  ISBN 0-201-00081-4

  ISBN 0-201-00082-2 (pbk.)

ISBN 0-201-00081-4-H
     0-201-00082-2-P
  FGHIJK-DO-8987654

Sixth Printing, April 1984

To Mondi

Acknowledgements

This book represents a personal inquiry into a confusing aspect of my own experience. My original intent was to make sense out of unexpected changes in my own life, and only after that to begin working with others who felt the same need—and only, then, belatedly to write a book. Hence my acknowledgements go not to people who helped me with a book or with a formal piece of research, but to people who helped me with my own transitions.

That represents a very large group of people, and I'm tempted to get out my address book and begin ticking off names. Instead, I want to thank four people who in different ways were essential to my quest for meaning. James Ingebretsen offered me support at a number of crucial points along the way, and John Levy was the good friend that I often needed. Mary Merrill helped me be believable to myself, and Mondi Bridges nudged and nurtured me all along the way. Having narrowed my debt down this far, I'll narrow it further still and dedicate this book to Mondi.

Contents

PART ONE

THE
NEED
FOR
CHANGE

The nine cities of Troy, each built on the ruins of its predecessor, were accumulated over millennia, from the Stone Age till Roman times. Pompeii was buried by volcanic eruption. . . . The Old World thus had its ghost towns, but more often than not they were buried and men built on the rubble of their ancestors' disappointed hopes. In America the archaeology of fast-moving men on a nearly empty continent was spread plain and thin on the surface. Its peculiar product was the abandoned place (the "ghost town") rather than the buried place. Its characteristic relics were things left by choice before they were used up.

DANIEL J. BOORSTIN
The Americans: The National Experience[1]

Americans have always been in transition. Whereas Old World families began with a place, New World families began with an act of migration. Nor did the transition from an old life to a new one end when the immigrants arrived on these shores. From place to place and job to job, they kept moving. Drawn forward by the faith that better things lay just beyond the horizon, they lived a life marked by frequent transitions. European visitors often noted that fact and marveled that Americans seemed to thrive on it. Alexis de Tocqueville, the great French student of American life, noted in his diary in 1831:

*Born often under another sky, placed in the
middle of an always moving scene, himself
driven by the irresistible torrent which draws
all about him, the American has no time to tie
himself to anything, he grows accustomed
only to change, and ends by regarding it as
the natural state of man. He feels the need of
it, more, he loves it; for the instability,
instead of meaning disaster to him, seems to
give birth only to miracles all about him.*[2]

That, at least, was one half of the American story—the
outer half. For inwardly this experience of being in transition was not so comfortable. Like old Rip van Winkle,
countless Americans "woke up" to the impact of change
on them at some point in their lives. Old Rip, you remember, had been put under a spell, so he had an excuse.
But for those who had been seeking transitions as a pathway to self-advancement the experience was very puzzling. At the age of fifty, Henry Wadsworth Longfellow, the
most famous American writer of his day, went back for a
visit to his hometown of Portland, Maine. While there, he
wrote a poem called "Changed," the opening stanzas of
which are:

From the outskirts of the town,
  Where of old the mile-stone stood,
Now a stranger, looking down,
I behold the shadowy crown
  Of the dark and haunted wood.

Is it changed, or am I changed?
  Ah! the oaks are fresh and green,

But the friends with whom I ranged
Through their thickets are estranged
  By the years that intervene.[3]

In the 120 years since that poem was written, the pace of change in American life has speeded up greatly. As Alvin Toffler wrote in *Future Shock,* "Change is avalanching upon our heads and most people are grotesquely unprepared to cope with it."[4] (That statement itself, being ten years old now, is presumably out of date!)

But it is not just the pace of change that disorients us. Many Americans have lost the old faith that all the transitions they are going through are really getting them anywhere. To be "up in the air," as one so often is in times of personal transition, is endurable if it *means something*—if it is part of a movement toward a desired end. But if it is not related to some larger and beneficial pattern, it becomes simply distressing.

Moreover, the experience of being in transition is itself changing. Being in between marriages or careers takes on a particularly painful quality when those things themselves are changing profoundly. It is as if we launched out from a riverside dock to cross to a landing on the opposite shore—only to discover in midstream that the landing was no longer there. (And when we looked back at the other shore, we saw that the dock we left from had just broken loose and was heading downstream.) Stuck in transition between situations, relationships, and identities that are themselves in transition, many Americans are caught in a semipermanent condition of transitionality.

One might imagine that writers and counsellors would have addressed themselves to this situation long ago. But that is not so. If you go to the library and look up "transition" in the subject index, you will probably find the headings skipping from "transit systems" to "translation"—nothing on transition. Of course, there are entries under "careers, changing," "divorce," and "bereavement," and a good deal is available on important specific life transitions, but there is nothing on the inner and underlying process that is common to all transitions.

4

There is, it is true, the current crop of books on adulthood, and they at least justify the difficulties one experiences: it's catch-30 or the mid-life debacle. But such books offer little real guidance. Combined with their idealized life-schedules, which fit like mail-order clothes, they do little to clarify the actual experience of being in the midst of transition.

That difficult process of letting go of an old situation, suffering the confusing nowhere of in-betweenness, and launching forth again in a new situation is the subject of this book. Drawing on current research into adult development, it suggests different ways of thinking about why transition occurs when it does. Recognizing that every lifetime has its own unique rhythm, *Transitions* provides the tools for identifying a personal developmental chronology. Cutting through the particulars of specific forms of change, it identifies the underlying process of personal transition and explains its characteristic impact on work and on relationships. Finally, it provides concrete ways for people to help themselves deal constructively with times of transition in their lives.

Transitions is not simply a manual on how-to-cope, however, for it is based on a theory of personal development that views transition as the natural process of disorientation and reorientation that marks the turning points of the path of growth. Throughout nature, growth involves periodic accelerations and transformations: Things go slowly for a time and nothing seems to change—until suddenly the eggshell cracks, the branch blossoms, the tadpole's tail shrinks away, the leaf falls, the bird molts, the hibernation begins. With us it is the same. Although the signs are less clear than in the world of feather and leaf, the functions of transition times are the same. They are key times in the natural process of self-renewal.

1

BEING IN TRANSITION

"Who are you?" said the
Caterpillar. . . .

"I—I hardly know, Sir, just at
present," Alice replied rather shyly,
"at least I know who I *was* when I
got up this morning, but I think I
must have been changed several
times since then."

LEWIS CARROLL
Alice's Adventures in Wonderland[1]

I first became interested in the subject of transition, in
the early seventies, when I was going through some difficult inner and outer changes. Although leaving my teaching career was one of these changes, I soon found myself
teaching a seminar called "Being In Transition." (Rule
number one: You find yourself coming back in new ways
to old activities, when you're in transition.) The twenty-
five adults who showed up for that course were in various
states of confusion and crisis, and I was a bit at sea myself. I had, after all, left my career and moved my family to
the country where we joined some other families to form a
small community; I had set out to change my life-style.

I had imagined, I think, that the seminar would at-
tract mostly other exurbanites and that we could puzzle
out together this difficult transition in our lives. There
were a few of these new country folk in the class, but the
mix was far richer than that. There were men and women
who were recently divorced or separated. There were a
couple of people who were newly married or remarried,
one a twenty-six-year-old man who had suddenly acquired
a full-scale, ready-made family of four kids. There was a
widow and several recently retired men. There was the
wife of a retired man (who didn't come himself because he

8

wasn't well enough, as his health had worsened suddenly a few weeks after his retirement).

There was a woman who had just had her first baby, a man who had just had a heart attack, and even a man who had just received a big promotion at work. ("What is *he* doing here?" the others asked resentfully. "*He* doesn't have problems.") There were three or four women who had just returned to college after years of child-raising. There were two people who had just been fired. And there was a young woman who was living on her own for the first time. She was appalled that the rest of us, her elders, didn't have our lives in better shape. "It's OK to be messing around when you're twenty-three," she said, "but I plan to get it all together by the time I'm your age." (We all nodded sheepishly and admitted that that had been our plan too.)

At first the seminar members were shy with each other and took refuge in the claim that they did not really have very much in common. ("*You* still have your job." "Well, *you're* luckier. You still have your marriage.") But slowly they began to discover that under the surface, their situations provided them with the same basic experience. As we listed them on the board the first night, the three main similarities seemed to be that each of us had experienced (1) an ending, followed by (2) a period of confusion and distress, leading to (3) a new beginning, in the cases that had come that far.

Each person's attitude toward what we began talking about as the three phases of transition differed considerably, of course. Those who had chosen their transitions tended to minimize the importance of the endings, almost as if they felt that to acknowledge that an ending was painful would be to admit that the transition was a mistake. On the other hand, those who had gone into transition unwillingly or unwittingly found it very hard to admit that a new beginning and a new phase of their lives might be at hand. They were as invested in seeing no good in their transition as the other group was in denying any distress. But all of them agreed that the in-between place was strange and confusing. They hoped to get out of it, in favor of either the Good Old Days or the Brave New World, as quickly as possible.

We decided to study these three phases of transition and I announced that *endings* would be the topic of our next class. This dismayed the young mother with the new baby. "I'm not sending him off to college," she said, "just trying to get used to having him." It was beginnings, not endings, that she was trying to cope with. He was, of course, a *wonderful* little baby (she repeated that several times), but she was having some small problems. How much should she let him cry, she asked her classmates, and how could she get her husband to help her more?

In seconds, the air was thick with advice and we were drifting away from *endings* fast. Interestingly enough, though, our advice quickly turned out to be of little use, for she had heard it all before—had even read most of it before the baby arrived. This upset her and she grew angry. First at her husband, and then at her mother who hadn't told her what mothering was really like, and then at the baby, and finally at us for "sitting there and nodding and acting sympathetic, when you don't give a damn if I'm falling apart—and I *am* falling apart!"

It was clear that we had come a long way from that *wonderful* little baby that she needed a little advice about. But we also seemed to be getting somewhere, for in the next few minutes she talked very movingly about her life and her dreams about motherhood. She and her husband had been married for two years before she got pregnant, and they had been very happy together. Both of them had wanted children, but each of them was startled to find a fussy new infant so intrusive and demanding. "We aren't alone together any more," she said sadly, after her anger had passed. "I really do love the baby, but the old freedom and easiness are gone. We can't take off any longer whenever we please or even live by our own schedules."

This woman, who had wanted us to forget endings and get on to beginnings, was being confronted with the impact of an ending on her life. The problems that we hadn't been able to solve for her were not so important, for no matter what happened to them, the underlying situation would remain. "I never thought of it this way," she said, "but now it seems to me that I crossed some kind of threshold in my life, and there's no going back. My old life is gone. How come nobody talks about that? They congratulate you on your new life, but I have to mourn the old life alone."

In fact this wasn't so. For as soon as she put her predicament into words, half a dozen people echoed her experience and gave their versions of it. So why was it so hard to talk about? For some people it was the shame they felt at being sad or angry at a supposedly "good thing." For others it was remorse over lost opportunities. And for still others it was simply the confusion and embarrassment over not being able to manage an ordinary life experience smoothly—something they imagined that others managed easily. For all these reasons, they found it difficult to speak about the unexpected impact of an ending in their lives—and the way in which that unacknowledged ending stood in the way of moving forward successfully toward a new beginning.

And thus we came to rule number two: Every transition begins with an ending. We have to let go of the old thing before we can pick up the new—not just outwardly, but inwardly, where we keep our connections to the people and places that act as definitions of who we are. There we are, living in a new town, with our heads full of all the old trivia: where the Chinese restaurant was (and when it opened in the evening), what Bob's phone number was, what shoe store had the children's sizes, and when the doctor took his day off. No wonder that those tribal rites of passage in which the group facilitates a person's transition from one life-phase to the next often contain rituals for clearing the mind of old memories and information.[2]

We usually fail to discover this need for an ending until we have made most of our necessary external changes. There we are, in the new house or on the new job or involved in the new relationship, waking up to the fact that we have not yet let go of our old ties. Or worse yet, *not* waking up to that fact, even though we are still moving to the inner rhythm of life back in the old situation. We're like shellfish that often continue to open and close their shells on the tide-schedule of their old home waters, even when they have been transplanted to the laboratory tank or the restaurant kitchen.

Why is this letting go so hard? This is a puzzling question, especially if we have been looking forward to a change. It is frightening to discover that some part of us is still holding on to what we used to be, for it makes us wonder if the change was in fact a bad idea. Can it be that the old thing was somehow (and in spite of everything we thought we knew) right for us and the new thing wrong?

These questions particularly arise when a person's life situation is not an especially happy one. The full-time mother who finally decides to break the narrow bounds of housecleaning and carpooling with a part-time job, or the bored office worker who gets a chance to join the staff of a newly formed company—these people will hardly expect to find the old roles hard to let go of. And the person who has been estranged from parents or siblings for years won't expect to be profoundly shaken by their deaths. How can we feel a "loss" when we marry after years of loneliness or get an inheritance after struggling to make ends meet or achieve fame after a career spent trying to make it?

The old radio comedian, Bob Burns ("The Arkansas Traveler"), used to tell the story of eating Army food for the first time after eighteen years of his mother's deep-fat frying. A week of the bland GI fare was enough to cure something that he had never known that he had: a lifelong case of heartburn. But rather than feeling relief at this improvement, Burns said that he rushed into the dispensary, clutching his stomach and yelling, "Doc, doc! Help me! I'm dying. My fire went out!"

We feel these unexpected losses because to an extent that we seldom realize, we come to identify ourselves with the circumstances of our lives. Who we think we are is partly defined by the roles and relationships that we have, both those we like and those we do not. But the bonds go deeper even than that. Our whole way of being—the personal style that makes you recognizably "you" and me "me"—is developed within and adjusted to fit a given life pattern. The very complaining that we do is part of that style. To hear Marge talk about Jack's inattentiveness or to hear Jack talk about never really being given a chance to show his stuff at work, you would think that they would jump at the chance to change. But then Jack brings home flowers, and Marge says, "What's wrong? I know that something's wrong!" And Jack gets an important assignment of his own and finally has the chance to get the attention that he has sought so long, and he finds several things wrong with the deal.

Jack may say to Marge (or the boss may say to Jack), "See, you really don't want to change. You like to gripe, but when you get the chance, you mess it up or chicken out." And that is half true—but only half. For the wanting is true, too, and the desire for change is also really true. Transitional situations bring this paradox to the surface—forcing us to look at both the negative and the positive aspects of our life situations.

There are ways of facilitating transitions, and they begin with recognizing that letting go is at best an ambiguous experience. They involve seeing transition itself in a new light and understanding the various phases of the transition experience. They involve developing new skills for negotiating the perilous passage across the "nowhere" that separates the old life situation from the new. But before that can be done, you need to understand your own characteristic ways of coping with endings.

One way to do this is to think back over the endings in your own life. Go all the way back to your early childhood and recall the earliest experiences that you can remember that involved endings. Some may have been large and terrible—deaths in the family, for instance—while others may have been insignificant to everyone except you—like your parents' departure on a trip or the death of a pet or a friend moving away. Continue this tour of your life history, beginning back then and coming forward, noting all the endings you can recall along the way. Some were physical, some involved relationships inside the family and out; some involved places, social groups, hobbies, interests, or sports, while others involved responsibilities, training, or jobs. Some endings may be hard to describe; they have few outward signs but they may leave long-lasting scars: the ending of a kind of innocence or trust, for example, or the ending of irresponsibility or of a religious faith. How many such endings can you retrieve from your memory?

As I said, we all develop our own typical response to ending things. The inner element in that response is a mental state or mood or frame of mind. Like the air we breathe, that mood can be so familiar as to be very difficult to identify. But it helps to think back on old endings and to try to recall the feelings and thoughts you had then. As you begin to remember your old reactions to endings, you are likely to find that your old mind-set is reactivated in the present whenever something ends in your life. Leaving for a better job may, ironically enough, cause the same grief and confusion that occurs when you reach the sad end of a core relationship. It is important to recognize this, for it means that some of the feelings you experience today have nothing to do with the present ending but come, instead, from old associations.

What you bring with you to any transitional situation is a style that you have developed for dealing with endings. The product of both early experience and later influence, this style is your own way of dealing with external circumstances and with the inner distress that they stir up. Your style is likely to reflect your childhood family situation, for transitions tend to set different family members off on different tasks: one person feels all the grief and anxiety for the whole group, another comforts the griever, another takes over the routine, while yet another goes into a sort of a parody of "being in control of the situation."

Somewhere along the way you may also have picked up somebody else's style to copy or adapt to your situation. Do you remember, for instance, Woody Allen's Humphrey Bogart "ending" in *Play It Again, Sam,* which consisted of saying "Sssso long, ssssweetheart," and then lighting a cigarette and walking off alone into the night?

Looking back over your ending experiences, what can you say about your own style of bringing situations to a close? Is it abrupt and designed to deny the impact of the change, or is it slow and gradual? Do you tend to be active or passive in these terminal situations? That is, is it your initiative that brings things to term or do events just happen to you? Some people learn early to cultivate a

15

subtle sort of receptivity to coincidence, or they become skilled at inviting others covertly to act upon them when change is in the wind.

Such people are characterized by a kind of blamelessness in regard to endings. They had no choice, they seem to say. The situation was beyond their control. In that first class on transition, we had several blameless ones, and they irritated everyone. None of us were feeling quite like the captain of our fate, but most of us acknowledged having played some part in the transition we were experiencing. Not the blameless ones, though, and particularly not one man whose wife had recently left him. ("She just walked out—no warning, no nothing—just left me.") He resented the idea that his own style might be one of inviting endings. He figuratively showed us his hands. ("See—clean.") And like someone who shouts "I didn't do it" when the police arrive, he called attention to himself and made everyone suspicious. He never caught on to what the others meant, and he finally stopped coming to class—another ending that he couldn't help—when one of the women *insulted* him by calling him "emotionally accident-prone." Rule number three: Although it is very advantageous to understand your own style of endings, there is some part of you that will resist that understanding as though your life depended on it.

If this process of recollection activates that part of you, you'll find it hard to remember past endings or to see any characteristic way you have of responding to them. Let that be. Just note your difficulty and try a different approach to the same question. Think about how you tend to act at the end of an evening at a friend's house or out on the town. Do you try to drag things out by starting new conversations and activities as others seem to be ready to leave, or do you say suddenly that it was a nice evening and dash out? Or what about some recent larger ending: leaving a job or moving from a neighborhood. Did you go

16

around to say goodbye to everyone, or did you leave a day ahead of schedule just so that you could avoid the good-byes?

Everyone finds endings difficult, so your own style is not a sign that you have some "problem" that others don't have. Both the person who leaves early and the one who stays late are avoiding endings and the discomfort of fac-ing the fact that there is a break of some sort in the con-tinuity of things. Whether you are a dasher or a lingerer is largely the result of how you learned to avoid the party's-over experience as a child. You may, on the other hand, have learned back then that there are unavoidable end-ings, but that they do not usually bring unendurable dis-tress and that dealing with them at the time avoids difficulty later. In that case, you are likely to try to take the experience one step at a time, saying your goodbyes and moving on to whatever comes next.

However you have learned to deal with them, endings are the first phase of transition. The second phase is a time of lostness and emptiness before "life" resumes an intel-ligible pattern and direction, while the third phase is that of beginning anew.

We will be discussing the in-between time in detail in Chapter 5, so we will move along here to the question of beginnings. You also have your own characteristic way of beginning things, and you can learn something about it by thinking back over your past, starting with early child-hood, just as you did with endings. Imagine that you were writing an account of your life. At what points could you use the phrase "A new chapter in my life opened when . . ."?

For some people these times of change and renewal always seem to involve new relationships, while for others they involve new places or projects. For still others it is some new state of mind that appears first, a new feeling or self-image or goal. Sometimes the beginning results from

17

careful and conscious effort, but for most people important new beginnings have a mysterious and sometimes accidental quality to them. That is interesting because most of us think that we ought to "take charge" of our lives and "plan carefully" when we're trying to get started after some ending. As we will see later, most of us do that prematurely, for our most important beginnings take place in the darkness outside our awareness. It is, after all, the ending that makes the beginning possible.

So we have rule number four: First there is an ending, *then* a beginning, with an important empty or fallow time in between. That is the order of things in nature. Leaf-fall, winter, and then the green emerges again from the dry brown wood. Human affairs flow along similar channels, or they would if we were better able to stay in that current. But endings are fearful. They break our connection with the setting in which we have come to know ourselves, and they awaken old memories of hurt and shame. Growing frightened, we are likely to try to abort the three-phase process of ending, lostness, and beginning. We even twist this pattern around so that beginnings come first, then endings, and then . . . then what? Nothing. It is when we turn things around in that way that transition becomes so unintelligible and frightening.

One of the benefits of reviewing your experience of endings is to see how often they have cleared the ground for unexpected beginnings. But reviewing these elements in your past may also turn up a number of times when the ending did not provide a starting point, as well as times when you started a new journey without unpacking your baggage from the old one. Right now, at this new transition point in your life, remember some of these aborted transition points from your past. Poke around among them as you might explore an old house you once lived in. Some of these unfinished transitions might still be completed, and you would bring more energy and less anxiety to your present situation as a result. Completion may involve no more than a belated farewell, a letter or a call to someone. It may involve an inner relinquishment of someone that outwardly you left behind years ago, or some old image of yourself, or some outlived dream or outworn belief that you have kept in your baggage long past its time. You'll travel more easily with some lightening of your load.

There is a great deal that most of us can do in finishing up with the past, but when we have done that we are back in the present, with all its ambiguities. In the midst of the change, it is not easy to say just what is ending and what else may emerge to take its place. One day everything seems to be coming apart, while the next day life goes on as usual, and we wonder if we have been imagining all our difficulties. We look around for some markers along the way to get our bearings by: How far have things actually changed, and what is the real result of the change on our lives?

One of the reasons that it is so difficult to assess these things is that the impact of transition upon us does not necessarily bear any relation to the apparent importance of the event that triggered it off. One person may be brought to a complete standstill by a divorce or a job loss, while another person may take it in stride. Someone else may come to terms with a debilitating illness and then be demolished at the loss of a beloved pet.

In that first transition class, I learned more about what accounts for these differences from the case of the class member whose only apparent life change was his promotion at work. He was in great distress, although he could not account for that fact, and the rest of the class tended to make light of it. The promotion itself was working out well, he claimed, but there was still some nameless change that threatened to wreck his whole life. We ran through the obvious categories: his finances were stable, his health was generally good, his kids were doing well in school, his career was going fine. "Nothing's wrong," he said irritably, and the rest of the class eyed him suspiciously, as though he might be a spy.

But then, as we got past the idea of "a promotion" to the reality of his life situation, a different picture began to emerge.

The promotion was just the tip of the iceberg, for in fact the man's company had undergone a major reorganization. The man's office had been shifted to a newly created division of the company, and his old boss, who had also been a good friend, had been fired. The man's new position required him to report to a whole new set of superiors, and he was not yet sure what they thought of him. "I keep wondering if they'll hang on to me long enough to get through the changes and then fire me too," he said.

The new job had two immediate effects on his home life. First, it required him to work longer hours, and second, it gave him a big pay raise. The new income, together with a mortgage that he hated to take, led to a major remodeling job at home. "I don't like the way we're suddenly spending so much more, and I try to explain that to my wife, but she just says that we've waited and waited for this, and now we ought to enjoy it." Life at home was, in fact, punctuated by many more arguments than in the past. He disapproved of her spending, and she disapproved of his new work schedule.

The longer hours had repercussions elsewhere as well. His kids complained that the family never did anything together any more, and his in-laws objected to the fact that he was always too busy to bring the family down for visits. Everyone objected to the way he now wanted to spend his spare time, for his new business associates encouraged his old interest in golf, which effectively brought an end to family camping trips.

"Then, just after I got the promotion, I got sick," the man said with a weary shake of the head. "Some timing! It was some strange virus, and it hung on for weeks. And then, of course, there was my brother's death. . . ." His voice trailed off, and he just sat there looking very tired.

"It's like a row of dominoes," another member of the class said, and all of us looked at the man with new compassion. The promotion had set off a tremor across the face of his whole life, leading to inner reorientations that were hard for the man to put into words. His brother's unexpected death at forty-eight and his own illness combined to undermine the man's old sense of invulnerability. The firing of his friend had the same effect, for it was not incompetence but organizational needs over which he had no control that had sent the man packing. "I've never felt this way before," the man said at the end of the evening, "but I feel as though my whole life was built on a frozen lake. We all go on with our activities. We work on the house and play golf and entertain and have our fights. I put in long hours at work and think I'm doing well. Then every once in a while I think, 'This is ice I'm standing on, and it's melting'—or 'Was that a crack I heard just then?' I try to forget, but I keep thinking, 'Damn, that ice looks thin!'"

This man was in a time of profound personal transition, one of those times of important realignment that punctuate each life on a few occasions. Under the deceptively smooth surface of a good job and a comfortable home, he was fighting for his life. He wanted the promotion, but he longed for the easier life he had left behind. His transition was one that anyone would have called "good," but it threatened to undermine his whole life as completely as death or disaster or any other "bad" change. The transition began at one place in his life, but its effects reached across every aspect of his world.

Few people stop to reflect, as this man had to, on the radiating waves of change in their lives. When they do, they may find that apparently minor events have had major impacts. They may find that puzzling and hard-to-identify distresses that they are feeling can be traced back to incidents or situations that set off the transition process in their lives. Sometimes they involve new beginnings that require unforeseen endings. Sometimes they involve endings with no new beginning in sight. The big events—divorce, death, losing a job, and other obviously painful changes—are easy to spot. But others, like marriage, sudden success, and moving to your dream house, are forgotten because they are "good events" and therefore not supposed to lead to difficulty. We expect to be distressed at illness, but it is a shock to find recovery leading to difficulty. We know that overwork is hard, but how can a big vacation lay us low? And how shall we account for the puzzling chains of events, none of which are especially big or traumatic, that make our lives look like Rube Goldberg machines, with one piece setting another into motion and the end result being way off in the corner somewhere. When a child enters school, a woman is free to take an outside job, and that additional money makes possible the first big vacation in years—at which time the husband decides to change jobs. It's not very elegant mechanics, but it is in fact the way life works.

We'll go on shortly to ways of understanding these distresses and the way that they seem to cluster at certain times in the life cycle, but for now it is important for you to think as clearly as you can about your own life situation. What are the events that have brought change into your life in the past year? And what are the areas of your life in which the changes are evident? Here are some categories and guidelines to help you to answer those questions.

Losses of relationships. What relationships have gone out of your life in the past year—list everything from a spouse's death to a friend moving away. Include marital separations, children leaving home, or the alienation of a former friend. What about the death of a pet, or the loss of some admired hero, or anything that narrows your field of relationships?

Changes in home life. Getting married or having a child; having a spouse retire, become ill (or recover), return to school, change jobs, or go into a depression; moving to a new house or remodeling the old one; experiencing increased (or decreased) domestic tension—anything that changed the content or quality of life in your home.

Personal changes. Getting sick (or well again); experiencing notable success (or failure); changing your eating habits, sleep-patterns, or sexual activities; starting or stopping school; changing your life-style or your appearance markedly.

Work and financial changes. Getting fired, retiring, or changing jobs; changes within your organization; increase or decrease in income; taking on new loans or mortgages; discovering that career advancement is blocked.

Inner changes. Spiritual awakening, deepening social and political awareness, or psychological insights; changes in self-image or values; the discovery of a new dream or the abandonment of an old one; or simply one of those nameless shifts which cause us to say, "I'm changing."

Two doctors named Thomas Holmes and Richard Rahe made a list of these kinds of events and worked out a point system to record the relative impact of each event on a person. The points range between 100 for the death of a spouse and 11 for a minor violation of the law. Thousands of people have taken this test, and their scores have been correlated with their health during the ensuing year or two. The results are startling. A score of less than 150 points puts you in an "average" group, with one chance in three of experiencing a serious health change in the next two years. (On the average, an American has a one-in-five chance of being hospitalized during this length of time.) If you score 150 to 300 points, your chances of such health changes rise to fifty-fifty. And if you score over 300 points, as the man with the promotion unexpectedly did, the odds for serious illness in that ensuing two-year period rise to almost nine-in-ten.[3]

No wonder the man with the promotion got the virus! No wonder so many people find their situations complicated by illness shortly after retirement. It makes you wonder about the frequency of colds during honeymoons and during the first week of school. And it makes you realize that transition takes its toll on us physically as well as mentally and socially.

It also makes you realize that there *are* times in everyone's life that are transitional in more than a quantitative sense. Events pile up outside us, and we respond inwardly in ways that leave us changed. Not all transitions affect us deeply, of course, but some endings do close out a whole chapter in our lives, while some beginnings open new ones. It is almost as though we did privately and according to our own schedule what tribal groups once did publicly according to a prescribed timetable: going through the process of passage between one life-phase and the next in a pattern of death and rebirth.

Since the publication in 1976 of Gail Sheehy's *Passages,* a number of studies have appeared that purport to tell us what the natural stages of adulthood are and where the characteristic times of transition can be expected to occur. My work with individuals in transition makes me believe that in a culture as diverse as ours, no one model of adulthood fits everyone—or even anyone—exactly. Yet you can catch glimpses of yourself in all of them, and so they are worth drawing upon in the task of charting out the course of your own life.

It is to that task that we now turn, for unless a particular time of personal transition is seen in the context of the individual life journey, it is unlikely to have any meaning larger than "ending this and starting that." It is, after all, that larger meaning that we are looking for when we ask *why*. "Why is this happening to me?" we wonder as we struggle to navigate the currents of transition. "And why now?" It is to those questions that we now turn.

2

A LIFETIME OF TRANSITIONS

What animal walks on four feet in
the morning, two feet at noon, and
three feet in the evening, yet has only
one voice?
The riddle of the sphinx

The human being.
Oedipus's solution to the riddle

The riddle of the sphinx was no mere test of wit, for it
imparted valuable wisdom concerning how a person
"stands" in the world. The riddle represents a scheme in
which there are two pivotal transition points. The first is
the turning point symbolized in the phrase walking "on
your own two feet"—that is, the transition from dependency to separateness and independence. The second
turning point, coming somewhere in the afternoon of life,
is symbolized by the acquisition of the cane or staff—a
transition that in the context of the mythic story of
Oedipus is not simply the coming of physical decrepitude
but is connected with a whole cluster of changes that
includes suffering and deepened insight and disengagement from an outlived way of living.

Compared to our current theories of adult development, this image of the course of life may seem simplistic.
We miss Erikson's "identity crisis" in adolescence, and
Sheehy's "trying twenties," Levinson's "settling down" in
the thirties—and what about the notorious "mid-life
crisis"? These theories about adult development are all
worth studying, but they do not invalidate the importance
of the sphinx's riddle. What the riddle reminds us is that
the lifetime has three natural and different phases and
that each has its own characteristic style. Further, it's
context—the story of Oedipus—suggests that the transi-

tion from one phase to the next is very difficult and involves certain problems.

In this chapter our task is to look at these transitions as they develop over the course of a lifetime. Only in this context does transition really make sense, for it is simply the way in which the individual's life moves on and unfolds. The ending-then-beginning pattern represents the way that a person changes and grows, and although one may not want to think about larger issues while in the immediate turmoil of transition, they must finally be dealt with if one is to understand not only what is happening but why, when, and how it is happening. In other words, I am not telling you to stop bailing—just to cast an eye over toward the map and to think about where you're headed.

Neither of the transition points identified in the sphinx's riddle is likely to be negotiated by a person in a single period of change. The transition from dependency to independence, for example, is likely to include gradually increasing degrees of separation between the individual and the parental world as well as various inner changes of values and identity by which the person develops his or her own self-image and outlook. Nor is this process complete when one leaves home or turns twenty-one: At thirty, forty, or even fifty we are likely to be still making the changes that complete the great life-transition to personal independence.

But long before we have finished with that transition we begin to encounter the first signs of the second great life-transition. "I can't be getting old yet!" exclaimed one of the men in the transition class only half-humorously. "I'm still struggling with my adolescence!" And we all knew how he felt. But the fact remains that sometime in our thirties, we are likely to note a shift in the wind that bespeaks a new weather system. The main storms are still well off beyond the horizon, but it is time to begin turning our attention away from the old issues of life's morning and toward those of the afternoon.

This whole theory, with its assertion of lifelong development and its claim that problems are often signals of life transitions, runs counter to modern views about adulthood. Those views come from a mechanistic theory about human beings that is being challenged on many fronts. Surrounded as we are by industrial products, we have tended to treat everything as if its essential nature were that of a product. In other words, like our cars, we people have our times of production and function and falling apart.

This outmoded view of the lifetime deserves a moment of our attention, for we need to understand its implications if we are not to fall back into it unwittingly. According to this view, human development is comparable to mechanical production—it begins with the period when the item is not yet "done," and it ends when the item is ready to "use." Any changes that occur after that point are "malfunctions" and signs that the mechanism needs repair. Whatever is done then involves finding some faulty part, just as the production process involved putting together the parts in the "right way." With cars, you start with the chassis, then add and assemble the pieces, attach the outer body and then paint it. And with people, we imagine, something similar goes on—with this training and that experience and that influence, one after the other, all adding up to the finished person, twenty-one years old and ready to roll.

The idea that de-velop-ment (which means "unfolding") continues uninterruptedly throughout the whole lifetime is entirely foreign to the world of products. Think how strange it would be to have an automobile mechanic lift the hood of your car and say, "Hey, see that swelling on the side of the cylinder block? That's your second carburetor beginning to sprout." Machines don't do that.

VW's do not turn into Volvos when they are five years old, nor do they grow a fifth gear at 45,000 miles. The rattle and clanking are not a sign that an old transition is still being completed or that a new transition is beginning. They're simply a sign that something is wrong with the car and it needs to be fixed.

Now we are beginning to understand that the production analogy has led to serious misunderstandings of our real nature and that we need a new way of thinking about the life cycle. No sooner did we begin to realize this lack than a number of books appeared in the bookstores on "adult development." The trend began in the early seventies with a few books on middle age, and by 1976 the floodgates were opened by Gail Sheehy's *Passages*. Subtitled, "The Predictable Crises of Adult Life," the book promised to make sense out of the changes that we were beginning to realize we were all going through. Then Sheehy's two main experts published their own books: Roger Gould came out with *Transformations: Growth and Change in the Adult Years* and Daniel J. Levinson published *The Seasons of a Man's Life*. And a dozen journalists have turned out books on some newly identified point of crisis or some decade. You would think that this previously uncharted territory would be pretty well mapped by now.

And it has been, although like those early maps of America, some of the explorers put the river here and some put it there and some said that there was no river. In other words, there is no shortage of theory—just considerable discrepancy between theorists. That's where the sphinx comes to our rescue, for when you start with the basic three-phase life image, then you can draw on current theory to suggest different aspects of each phase and why a particular time of transition involves the particular issues that it does. In so doing, we will see that the force of life's two great developmental shifts fan out over the whole lifetime, with the first one involving an end to old dependencies and the establishment of the person as a separate social entity, and the second one involving movement beyond that separateness to something more complex, to a deeper sense of interrelatedness. The whole middle third of life is characterized by a mixture of these different influences. While the particulars cannot be pinned down chronologically, you will be able to find their location in your own life history.

Let's go back to a beginning before adulthood starts—the turning point at the end of childhood. Our culture is too individualistic to have standardized the experience, as most earlier cultures did, but you will have unique associations to the phrase, *the end of childhood.*

The end of childhood. What does that phrase recall from your past? Your first sexual experience, perhaps, or a move to a new town. You might date it from the beginning of some new interest or from the ending of some old relationship. Or you may associate it with some less clear-cut change—no big event, no particular situation, just the sense, as you walked home alone from school or sat looking out of your bedroom window, that you weren't the same any more, that childhood had disappeared like yesterday's weather.

Modern tribal societies place tremendous emphasis on this transition point, as did ancient civilizations. The entire maturation process is compressed into one dramatic event and the occasion is used to facilitate the transformation of the person from dependency to independence. Furthermore, the coming of age rituals set the tone for a lifetime of celebrations of subsequent transformations.

It's worth reflecting on this early transition point in your own life because that point may have set the style for your own later transitions. That was the case with me, I think. At the end of grammar school, I happened to move from a very small town to a medium-sized city and from a

little school to a big one. My old friends had been un-
sophisticated kids, for the most part, and I felt at home
with them. But then suddenly I was in school with children who paid attention to what they wore and knew
about city life and moved with the times. I had to change
my whole way of life in order to fit in, and for some time I
felt like a displaced person. It is probably no accident that
I tend to view my own life transitions as shifts in life-style
and to associate them with physical moves.

It was quite different for Joanna, a fortyish member of
the transition class. She had been separated from her
husband for several months and was so immobilized by
the change that she hardly spoke during the first weeks of
the class. As she said later, she was holding on to her past
and refusing to start life anew as a single person. It was
almost as though she didn't know how to let go or as if she
were waiting for some signal.

Then one night in class she started to talk. A terrible
thing had happened that week, she said. She had been
driving along a winding road in the evening and, coming
around a corner, she had been momentarily blinded by the
lights of an oncoming car. Swerving to avoid it, she had
run off the road.

The car had been badly damaged and she had been
cut and bruised. But she had somehow also been set into
motion, for in the next few days she had found a part-time
job and moved in with a friend to save money. And now
she was beginning to talk to her classmates for the first
time.

It was a terrible experience, she kept repeating. She
might have killed that other driver. "I know what it does to
a person to be responsible for somebody's death," she said,
and she began to cry. "I saw what it did to my mother. It's
an incredible coincidence, really, but when I was thirteen
my whole world was changed by another automobile accident. My mother was driving us all to school one morning,

and she didn't see a stoplight and ran into a big truck. My sister was very badly hurt, and I was out of school myself for a while."

We all sat there stunned, as much by her sudden volubility as by the coincidence of her misfortune. She went on to say that her mother had become very depressed after the accident and had, in effect, stopped taking care of the house. Joanna herself had to take over the responsibilities of cooking and cleaning. "I was forcibly evicted from childhood. That accident did it," she said.

Did Joanna contrive to reenact this terrible event to terminate another chapter in her life, we all wondered? Or did the ending that she needed to make remain unrealized until the right event came along to bring it to the surface? There are no simple answers to these questions, and they may not be mutually exclusive. The point is that Joanna and I (and quite possibly you) had a memorable transition experience around the end of childhood, and that experience was established in our awareness as a model for life transitions. Lacking formal rites of passage and guidance in these matters, it is not surprising that the basic form of that experience or elements from it may reappear later in our lives.

The ending of childhood is one part of the shift from life's morning (or dependency) to life's noon (or independence). A second part of that shift involves establishing a separate identity, distinct from that of so-and-so's child. In traditional societies the new identity was partly prescribed by the person's status and clan and partly discovered in the course of the rite of passage, when some guardian spirit or ancestor or guru gave the person a new name and a new sense of destiny. With us the old prescriptions have largely broken down, and we have fallen back on the idea that an identity is assembled during youth.

The psychologist Erik Erikson has explained how that process of identity formation works during youth,[1] when a person tries on a series of roles and experiments with different kinds of relationships. Daughter, good athlete, average student, girlfriend, actress, sister, babysitter, pal, shy person, closet moralist, dreamer—out of this potpourri of identities some coherent sense of self must be formed. This is the developmental business of youth, says Erikson, and what is called the *task* of this phase of life.

Every phase of life has such a task, and failing to complete it satisfactorily means that the person makes the transition into the next phase with unfinished business. And in fact most of us did only a passable job of resolving identity issues back then. Consequently, whenever we enter a new transition, some of those old identity issues are going to reemerge. "I feel like I'm sixteen again," said a woman in the transition class. "The divorce took away the main identity I'd had for six years, and I find myself now trying out different ways of being, different roles, almost different personalities, the way I did when I was a teenager." This had been a very disturbing experience for her, although after we talked about the way transition reactivates our old identity crises, she discovered that once she accepted her experience as natural, she rather enjoyed it.

Each member of a tribal group moves straight from childhood into adulthood, but most of us do not. Instead, in slowly changing forms, our dependency continues for some years. We eat the food our parents buy, we live in their house, we turn to them for help when we face some difficulty. But slowly all this changes and then one day we are finally on our own. That is the next important transition point for most people, the time when they leave home and set up shop for themselves. *On Your Own:* What memories and feelings do you associate with that phrase? You may think of moving into an apartment with several friends and getting your first real job, or you may think of a series of gradual shifts—going away to school (but remaining financially dependent), getting a part time job (but having to borrow money from your parents for graduate school), and finally finishing school and earning enough to settle your debts with your parents. Some people react sadly to thinking about being on their own: "I don't think I really made that transition," said a woman in the transition class. "Here I am at fifty, with my children flying the coop, and I'm only now beginning to taste what it's like to be on your own. I got married so fast after I left home that I just switched dependencies."

People's experiences vary greatly here. Charles Dickens was hardly more than ten when he began to work in a London blacking factory and had to live by his wits in a nearby slum. No unfinished business there—except that the insecurities created by this premature independence stayed with Dickens all his life. At the other extreme, I knew a man of seventy who lived with his parents and worked for his ninety-five-year-old father in the family business. No insecurities for him—that is, so long as he kept his life within the tiny circle of his familiar world from childhood and excluded alien experiences, like adult relationships and a real career. Those are extreme cases, of course, but most of us can find in our lives the vestiges of the transition to living on our own.

What comes next in this ongoing transformation of the dependent child into independent adult? As the initial excitement and panic of being separate from the parental orbit begin to wane, new questions begin to arise and the emphasis shifts from getting away from something to finding and fitting into something. This is what psychologist Daniel J. Levinson calls the phase of "entering the adult world."[2] Erikson says that the major developmental task is forging strong new interpersonal relationships and thereby exploring one's capacity for intimacy. In the broadest sense, we might say that this time is one of "searching for a place" and that the transitions that are likely to take place involve experimenting with situations with an eye to making commitments.

Some people move very quickly at this time. They get married, launch careers, and begin families. They find a place for themselves fast and make long-range commitments with very little experimenting. Others hang back, trying out several relationships and several jobs and several apartments. They leave school to work for a while, and then return to school after taking some time off to do nothing but travel. For these people the search for a place involves dozens of transitions spread out over ten years, while for others all the transitionality is telescoped into one grand leap into family life and a career.

In making this contrast, I am not suggesting that one way is better than the other. I only want to suggest how even very different life experiences actually reflect the same basic transitional task of shifting from the centrifugal force of leaving childhood to the centripetal one of finding a suitable place in the world. There is, in fact, no right way, for every way has its price and its rewards. The early place-finders may later regret that they did not see more of the world and come to know themselves better before making long-term commitments, while the experimenters may wonder whether they waited too long and missed some hidden moment when settling down would have felt just right and would have worked. Both groups tend to find themselves asking these questions as they approach thirty. Levinson calls this time the "age thirty transition," while Gould emphasizes a growing realism about oneself and calls it a time of "opening up to what's inside."[3] In either case, it seems to be a time of second thoughts.

This can be the pivotal transitional point in a lifetime. Whatever it was that people were doing before begins to seem not quite right. About a third of that first transition

class was within two or three years of thirty, and they
were struck with this coincidence, even though at first
they found it hard to see what else they had in common.
Anne was getting a divorce, while Mort announced that he
was at last getting ready to settle down. Some people had
just discovered meaningful work for the first time, while
others were ready to chuck good careers that they had
worked hard to launch. Sally, aged thirty-two, was starting
to think about how much longer she could safely have a
first child—and if, in fact, she really wanted children,
while Pat was set to let her former husband take full
custody of their child so that she could resume the career
that she had left to get married. The variety was immense.
But beneath the surface, the various transitions began
with the discovery that roles and relationships were starting to pinch and bind like somebody else's clothes.

"I can't even remember how I got into this damned
job!" said Tod with disgust to the rest of the class one
evening. "I went to graduate school to try to accomplish
something and make a difference in the world, and here I
am pushing papers all day, filling out forms that a high-
school kid could do. And the people at work! They don't
even know who I am—or care."

Jannine listened to this with a puzzled look. "This all
sounds strange to me because I've been envying your stability and security ever since the class began. I keep thinking, 'When does the Great Search end? Am I going to end
up an old woman who lives with her cats and who's never
stayed in one place more than two years?' I can hardly go
through a residential neighborhood any more without
wanting a house of my own so badly that I go home and
start counting my assets again. I'm tired of the quest and
the adventure."

Second thoughts can turn one's thirties into a very
difficult time. It is often the first time of transition after
leaving home orginially when a person feels real doubt

about the future. It can also be a very lonely time, since the very people that one would normally talk to about personal problems may be the people that one is having second thoughts about. And the distress is deepened by the old idea that if you did things right, you would have everything settled once and for all by twenty-five or so.

The source of this transitionality around thirty was first noted years ago by Charlotte Buhler, the Viennese psychologist. In her study of the biographies of hundreds of men and women, she found that although physical dependence on parents usually ended in the late teens, a really successful and long-lasting set of commitments were often not made until a person was almost thirty. The intervening years were likely to be spent in roles and relationships that were technically "adult" but were actually "preparatory [in] character" to what the person was actually going to do during the bulk of the adult years.[4]

Levinson's research on the lives of contemporary men and women suggests a similar thing, and he calls the years from twenty-two to thirty-three the "novice period" of adulthood. Perhaps it would be better if we viewed thirty rather than twenty-one as the first great watershed of the lifetime—or better yet, if we viewed the end of childhood, the time of being on one's own, the search for a place, and the time of second thoughts as a series of settings in which transitions accomplish the larger developmental business of transforming us from dependency to independence.

Throughout this novice period, transitions have a special poignancy and anxiousness about them, for they often seem to threaten a return to the old dependency. It is only a move to a new town or a new job, it is only breaking up a short-lived relationship—but whatever the case, it feels like you are going back to Go. "I have to start all over," said a thirty-year-old businessman-turned-teacher, "and I feel like I missed the first hour of the race. I'm going to have to run like hell to catch up." "You think *you've* had a setback," muttered a man in the class who had married at eighteen and was now, at twenty-eight, in the midst of a trial separation. "Hell, I feel like I'm still a teenager, and the next thing I know I'll start taking my laundry home to Mom again!"

It's important to recognize the reason for these feelings and to realize that they are natural. The fact that things are up in the air now and that you sometimes feel you are right back where you started is no sign that you have made a mistake or have been wasting your time for the past ten years. It is only a sign that you are in one of life's natural and periodic times of readjustment and renewed commitment. You are at the end of the novice period of adulthood, a time when long-term commitments (including the renewal of old commitments) are often made. You know the rules now, and you're beginning to sense what you can and cannot do well. They don't ask to see your driver's licence in the liquor store any longer. You are, for better or for worse, an undisputed grown-up. The question is, *now* what are you going to do?

How you handle the transitions that may be prompted by second thoughts can determine the course of your life for years to come. Having decided to repress inner promptings to change, some people begin at this point to turn away from the opportunities for development provided by transition and instead deal with these opportunities as temporary and accidental disruptions in an otherwise stable state of life. In the short run these people seem to gain by avoiding the time-consuming shifts and inner reorientations that others experience around thirty. But in the long run they lose—becoming the brittle beauties of the suburbs and the company yes-men who rejoin them at the end of the day.

But for many people this time of second thoughts provides a clearer sense of personal direction than they have hitherto known—and often some goal or project that embodies that direction. The thirties can be a time of new or renewed commitment to what Levinson calls "the tribe"—a social grouping that has particular importance for the individual. This can be a formal organization or a profession, the community where one lives or an ethnic population of which one is a part, or "men" or "women" or "the working class" or even "humankind." Although he is writing only about men, Levinson's words apply to both sexes: After the "age thirty transition" comes

> a time for a man to join the tribe as a full adult on terms he can accept: time to find his niche, get plugged into society with greater commitment and responsibility, raise a family and exercise an occupation and do his bit for the survival and well-being of the tribe. . . . [Whatever the person's particular "tribe,"] everyone during Settling Down is strongly connected to a segment of his society, responsive to its demands and seeking the affirmation and rewards it offers.[5]

This "settling down" can represent a major life transition if the person has remained transient through the novice phase of adulthood, although for people who keep their initial relationships and work-life intact, it can mean simply a slight reorientation and a renewed commitment after a time of reappraisal. I have the impression from the people whom I have worked with that those who tailor their situations to their own capacities and needs most carefully at this time make the most successful long-term commitments and that those who power their way through these shoals without much change are the ones who are heading for really rough times around forty. Be that as it may, this transition point sets the tone for much that follows in the middle decades of the lifetime.

It has been fashionable to highlight the next point of transition, to make it into the very center of the developmental design. Sometime around forty, so runs this argument, the skies darken and the seas rise and the crew casts worried glances toward the lifeboats. All ships head into the wind and prepare to ride out the most infamous of transitions—the mid-life crisis. (Sturm und Drang music, please.)

I used to subscribe to this theory, for I was just turning forty and in the midst of the changes that led to that first transition class when I began to try to make sense out of "adult development." But now, six years later, I see matters a little differently.

To begin with, the most important fact is not that there are one or three or six identifiable periods of crisis in the lifetime, but rather that adulthood unfolds its promise in a rhythm of expansion and contraction, change and stability. In human life as in the rest of nature, change accumulates slowly and almost invisibly until it is made manifest in the sudden form of fledging out or thawing or leaf-fall. It is the transition process rather than a thing called a mid-life transition that we must understand.

The second fact to remember is that not everyone finds life coming to a halt or standing on its head at forty. Rather, from the early thirties on, most people find life moving in a pattern of alternating periods of stability and change. The mid-life transition is the first of these transition times after the end of the novice period, and for many people it is a time of considerable upheaval. But not everyone makes the biggest changes then, "I'm having my mid-life crisis at fifty-five," Tom kept reminding us during the transition class. "I may be a little slow," he'd say leaning back in his chair, "but when I got there, I finally really let go!" (He had suddenly sold his furniture store the year before, and was now "into consciousness," whatever that meant.)

Another reason that it is misleading to single out the mid-life transition for such special treatment is that it is the result not of newly present factors in the lifetime but of a mixture of old and new ones. On the one hand, things are full of promise, while on the other hand they lack any meaning. On the one hand, the kids are almost grown, on the other hand, the parents are getting old. On the one hand, forty is the beginning and on the other hand, it's the end.

"It's the mirror that does it to you first, I think," said Betty on one of the final nights of the class. "I still thought of myself as I had been ten years earlier, but one day I looked in the mirror and said, 'Where'd you come from? What ever happened to Betty—the one that used to live here?'"

Within organizations, one begins to realize that there is a widening gap between oneself at forty and the younger employees. It is as though some unmarked boundary had been crossed unawares, and one is now in another country. The young and the old each seem to have their places in the structure, while the middle-aged have lost a sense of belonging.

It is no accident that such people should be ripe for a reassessment of the hopes and plans that brought them this far. Now is the time when the melancholy wit of Oscar Wilde hits home: "The Gods have two ways of dealing harshly with us—the first is to deny us our dreams, and the second is to grant them." When a person has realized a dream, the result is a puzzling sense of "Is this *it*? Is *this* what I've been trying to reach?" And when a person has failed to realize a dream—and it tends to be around this time that such discoveries are made—it becomes necessary to face what existential psychologist James Bugental has called "the nevers": "I guess that I'm never going to be the head of the firm . . . never going to have children of my own . . . never going to be the great writer . . . never going to be rich . . . never going to be famous." For many it is a time of coming to terms with the recognition that they have been chasing a carrot on a stick.

These discoveries are thought-provoking, to say the least, but they sometimes open the door to new activities and new achievements that were impossible under the old dreams. Carried free of the old conflicts and confusions of trying to make it, and carried out into the clear water of self-knowledge and service, many people find at last what they were meant to do and be. Gandhi discovered at fifty his real mission in nonviolent resistance. Cervantes was older than that when he began his career as a novelist. Lou Andreas Salome was over sixty when she became a psychoanalyst. And then there is Grandma Moses as well as Colonel Sanders.[6]

Some books offer roadmaps to the middle and later years, telling you what you ought to be doing when—or more likely, making you feel inadequate for not doing at fifty or seventy what they say you ought to be doing. But I think that is misleading; the whole idea of typical stages begins to break down as one enters the middle years. It is the business of constructing a separate and independent life that has stages, with first this and then that. The process of letting go of that style of living and discovering a different relation to things cannot so easily be reduced to fixed sequences. One has a sense of change, as with the weather toward the end of a season, but there seems to be no clear pattern, any more than there is with fall storms.

The transitions during this period depend less often on personal initiative and more often on someone else's actions, like your child's decision to leave home or to marry. As one grows older, the increasing number of illnesses and deaths among contemporaries carries with it the potential for unforeseen and unwanted transitions. Yet every transition is an ending that prepares the ground for new growth and new activities.

As life passes the second great point of transformation into the time in which the sphinx's image of the man with the staff is the dominant one, the person's own expectations become very important. These are largely the product of the person's culture and family history. In the Orient, old age is revered as life's apex—a time of greatest influence and deepest wisdom. The ancient Hindu image of the lifetime has an important transition point around the time of the birth of one's grandchildren. Until that time one has been in the "householder" stage of life, a time in which self-fulfillment and personal development have involved participation in social roles, family life, and the world of work. But now one is ready for a change—a change caught in the very name of the next life stage, that of the "forest dweller."

This important life-transition, for which we in the west have no real counterpart, comes when, in the words of religious historian Huston Smith,

> *the time has come for the individual to begin his true adult education, to discover who he is and what life is all about. What is the secret of the "I" with which he has been on such intimate terms all these years yet which remains a stranger? . . . What lurks behind the world's facade, animating it, ordering it—to what end?*[7]

As the name of this life stage suggests, the transition into it is one of turning away from the world's business and going into the solitude of the forest for a time of reflection and study.

This important shift during life's second half, which is not the same as our retirement because it is less a transition from something than a transition to something, corresponds to inward changes that are evident in many Americans. A growing concern for meaning and a loss of interest in simple performance is evident in many people after mid-life. One of the members of the transition class put it this way: "I took an early retirement, although it wasn't for the leisure as such that I did it. The idea of sitting on the beach or puttering in the garden doesn't appeal to me much, but I wanted to use the time to . . . well, think. That sounds funny, I guess. I never was any great brain, and I was so busy selling that I never read very much. But still, even though I can't exactly say why, I really want time to think now." Several of the older class members nodded in recognition.

This shift was common among the middle-aged and older patients of Swiss psychiatrist Carl Jung. Describing the typical outlook of such a patient, Jung wrote:

> *Social usefulness is no longer an aim for him,*
> *although he does not question its desirability.*
> *Fully aware as he is of the social*
> *unimportance of his creative activity, he*
> *looks upon it as a way of working out his own*
> *development.* [8]

The developmental process at this point seems to be akin to ripening. No wonder it has failed to show up on the measures of external change—except in negative terms as a loss of interest in external achievement.

The transitions of life's afternoon are more mysterious than those of its morning, and so we have tended to pass them off as the effects of physical aging. But something deeper is going on, something as purposive in its own way as the development of social roles and interpersonal rela-

46

tionships in life's first half. It involves letting go of a particular kind of self-image and style of coping with the world. Seldom done in any single time of transition, this is the developmental business of life's second half.

There exists, however, a great myth that clearly portrays this shift from life's morning to its afternoon, the change from two-leggedness to three. That is the myth of Odysseus, the Greek hero of the Trojan War. He is older than many of the other warriors, a middle-aged man with a wife and a nearly grown son back on the island of Ithaca. On a literal level the tale that bears his name tells about the mysterious setbacks that cause a three-week homeward voyage to become a ten-year journey; but on a deeper level it tells about another kind of journey. This is no simple trip, but rather the journey of personal transformation that becomes possible after an individual has done the world's business for long enough. Because this story tells so memorably about this homing process, it is worth recounting in some detail.

The story begins with difficulties. As Odysseus explains to anyone who will listen, they involve a terrible and unexpected defeat right after the enormous victory at Troy. Odysseus and twelve shiploads of men had put ashore at the little village of Ismaros. They had wanted just a little more loot and some wine for the trip home. To these brave victors from the plains of Troy, Ismaros looked like a pushover. But something happened. The soldiers took too long and drank too much; a neighboring tribe rode down out of the hills and caught them unawares, and these great warriors were sent limping back to their ships, beaten and wounded.

What had happened? What had gone wrong? This was the sort of thing that Odysseus had become famous for doing well—but this time it failed. The incident at Ismaros sets the tone for the whole story, for throughout the tale Odysseus discovers in one way and then another that he has crossed some mysterious line in his life and that everything that once worked for him now works against him. Like most of us, Odysseus is a slow learner—or *un*learner, for it turns out that his most difficult tasks are those of unlearning much that brought him to life's middle years and to the height of his renown.

Consider Odysseus's attempt to sail safely between Scylla and Charybdis, the monster and the whirlpool that have come to stand in the Western imagination for the impossible choices in life. The sorceress Circe had explained to him that he could negotiate the narrows only if he did not resist the dangers there. Odysseus demurred, announcing that he was *Odysseus* and would never turn away from combat. "You rash man," she replied. "Do the works of war concern you still, and toil? Will you not yield to the immortal gods?" But when he got to the narrow place in the journey, he "forgot the hard injunction of Circe, when she ordered me in no way to arm myself. I put on my famous armor, took two long spears in my hands, and went up on the deck of the ship at the prow." The little man standing on the deck of a fragile vessel, playing the hero when the time for heroism had passed!

It is significant that in this case (and others as well) Odysseus's help and insights came from women. In the *Illiad,* of course, everything had been male, but in the *Odyssey* it is to the wisdom of the opposite sex that he must turn to find the way. It is no accident, of course, that Odysseus's whole journey home is toward his feminine counterpart, Penelope. In symbolic terms, he is coming home to his own feminine side.

Poor Penelope, weaving and unweaving her cloth while the hundred suitors propositioned her and ate and drank everything in the house. If this were *her* story, you can bet that it would have been different. At forty she probably would have told everyone what they could do with that drafty old palace, and she might have had a fling with one of the suitors, too. She would have had her "exploring" to do, just as Odysseus did, and would have found much to learn from mentors of the opposite sex.

The point is that in life's homing phase and process, encounters with the powers of the opposite sex are symbolic in a sense that is different from life's first half. Carl Jung emphasized the same point when he wrote:

> *We might compare masculinity and femininity . . . to a particular store of substances of which, in the first half of life, unequal use is made. A man consumes his large supply of masculine substance and has left over only the smaller amount of feminine substance, which he must now put to use. It is the other way round with a woman; she allows her unused supply of masculinity to become active.*[9]

Odysseus goes through hell on his way home—as most of us do. And he does so in a different spirit from those underworld journeys taken by younger mythic heroes. His journey is not another exploit and not a test of his manhood, for Odysseus journeys into hell humbly and because it is necessary to his homecoming. He goes to learn what he needs to learn.

By that time, Odysseus has lost much of the brittle pride with which he began. The homeward journey has been marked by a process of constant attrition. First he had twelve ships, then only six and later only three. Finally he was down to one, manned by the few men who were left with him. And at the end he was alone, his last boat sucked down and ripped apart in the great whirlpool of Charybdis. Metaphorically he is stripped of the various supports on which he had earlier relied, a loss that is grievous but also one that leaves him able to know in a totally new sense who he really is.

In suffering this attrition, Odysseus learns a kind of courage that is different from the cunning and the aggressiveness of the battlefield. That courage is realized when his boat is caught in the whirlpool. Just as it is sucked down to destruction, he reaches up and grabs a branch of a fig tree that hangs over the water. With a new kind of bravery, he holds on, not knowing whether it will really matter or not, until suddenly the whirlpool regurgitates all that is left of his ship—the naked keel and the bare mast. Letting go at last of his painful hold, Odysseus drops athwart the keel and paddles with his hands out to sea. This king and hero, who began with a fleet of ships, leaves the scene like a child on a log.

This same stripping down process characterizes Odysseus's encounter with the giant Polyphemus, who returns unexpectedly to find Odysseus and his men exploring the cave where he lives. Blocking the entrance with immense boulders Polyphemus traps the warriors and begins eating them, two at a meal. Nevertheless, through ingenuity, Odysseus and his remaining troops soon manage to get free.

When Polyphemus discovers their escape, he calls to his neighboring giants for help, shouting that "Oudeis" has escaped. *Oudeis,* which was what Odysseus had called himself when he met the giant, is the Greek word for "nobody." So when Polyphemus shouts that nobody has injured him and that nobody is escaping, the other giants simply shake their heads and wonder what is wrong with their friend.

In the world of Greek heroes, Odysseus has just done an unusual thing—he has given up his identity. Identities meant fame, and fame meant power. Great heroes sometimes won combats simply by scaring off their opponents.

"I am Heracles . . . Achilles . . . the great Theseus." To
say, "I am Nobody" and to find in that new nonidentity a
source of power—that is something significant, and it
marks a stage of development going beyond the reliance
on roles and statuses that mark life's two-legged mid-day.
It is also no accident that the giant who opposes Odysseus
in this initiatory struggle carries the name Polyphemus,
meaning "famous" in Greek. For Odysseus has reached
the point in his development where he must begin to turn
back on himself those forces which he has been directing
outward at the world. It is the point at which the hero
must stop slaying dragons and begin to start slaying the
dragonslayer.

Throughout Odysseus's long journey home, he is confronted by one distraction after another, each of which
has its meaning in the context of life's second half. There
is the song of the Sirens, which symbolizes the self-
destruction lurking beneath the beguiling surface of all
that calls upon us to turn aside. There is the lotus fruit,
which stands for all that makes us forget the journey itself and our real destination. There is Calypso's promise: "Stay with me and you need never grow old." That
fantasy—that we can stop the on-going process of life
transitions—represents the most tempting and illusory
promise of all. In spite of lapses, Odysseus somehow
struggled past each blandishment as he struggled through
the batterings.

Not all the difficulties are passed even when Odysseus
finally lands in Ithaca. Things are a mess at home. The
rival princes are overrunning his palace, living off his
riches and usurping his rightful place. At the mythic level,
these interlopers correspond to all the inner confusions
and distractions that block our inner homecoming—all
those usurpers that move in to run things whenever our
awareness absents itself. Just as we are about to reclaim
the inner kingdom of selfhood, home at last from the long

journey, we discover not only that is there no welcoming committee on the dock to meet us but that we are going to have to fight our way into our own rightful place. So in the end, the homeward journey of life's second half demands three things of us: First, that we unlearn the whole style of mastering the world that we used to take us through the first half of life. Second, that we resist the longings to abandon the developmental journey and refuse the invitations to stay forever at some attractive stopping place. And third, that we recognize that it will take real effort to regain the inner "home."

The Odyssey is an important corrective to the view that most of us grew up with: that the years between twenty-five and sixty-five form an unbroken plain, and that people do not change significantly from the time that they get situated to the time that they retire. So too are the careers of those individuals who broke the unwritten rule that after forty it is all replay. Consider Joshua Slocum, who set out at fifty-one to sail around the world alone and made it three years later. And Handel, who was deeply in debt and struggling to recover from a stroke when he accepted at fifty-seven a commission to write a choral work for a charitable performance and produced *The Messiah*. And Edith Hamilton, who did not even begin her work as a mythographer until after she retired from teaching at sixty—and who inaugurated at ninety a series of four annual trips to Europe.[10]

The transitions of life's second half offer a special kind of opportunity to break with the social conditioning that has carried us successfully this far and to do something really new and different. It is a season more in tune than the earlier ones with the deeper promptings of the spirit.

Unfortunately, it is also a time when we are surrounded by distractions. In many cases, we're still actively involved with our careers, and the house may not be paid for—oh, yes, and the kids aren't done with college, and all of our security is tied up in the company's pension plan, and there'd be big taxes to pay if we sold the house now. Maybe we're coping with the climacteric or struggling across the burning sands of middle age. This is a hell of a bad time to start talking about new beginnings!

Perhaps. Certainly I'm not trying to provide another kind of prescription—a new change that we are all supposed to go through in unison at forty-five or sixty-five. Rather I want to argue for the idea that the path of aging is a unique journey for everyone who takes it. For the truth is that although ours is a youth-oriented culture, many of us do not come into our own until our lives are half or three-quarters over. Schopenhauer noted this over a century ago, writing that "each man's character seems best suited to one particular stage of life; so that he appears at his best in that stage of life."[11]

This suggests that whatever else transition may give to or take away from our lives, it leads us at some point into our own best time of life and then later leads us out of it again. How has it been for you? What would you say is your own natural stage of life? Were you born to be seventeen or seventy? Are you a perennial twenty-five-year-old, or are you still waiting for your entrance cue at fifty? One often hears evidence about these matters in discussions of which birthdays are hardest. There is always disagreement, for what is really being discussed is when some self-image went out of sync with the calendar. What has your own experience with this been?

Expand this recollection a little. Which of your own life transition points have been the most important so far? We have been discussing a whole series of typical times of transition and the developmental issues that are critical at each stage. But forget that. What is the chronology of your own experience with transition? Begin with the end of childhood and come up to the present. In some of these transitions, nothing very important changed. But in others, a chapter of your life ended. Make a list of these significant transitions.

When you have done this, begin with the early transitions and see what you can say about the "developmental issues" that were involved with each transition. When I did this, some of my entries were:

1951—17 years old: entered college; first time on my own; first real test of my abilities.

1955—21 years old: graduation; panic over career; decide to stay in school and avoid moment of decision; change of universities, but real transition avoided.

1956—22 years old: drafted into army; sudden entry into "the real world"; freedom from old expectations and self-image.

1958—24 years old: discharged; grappling again with the question of career.

And so on. Your chronology and the transitional events may be more decisive than mine were. Obviously, I found it very hard to get going on a career, and several of my transitions back then represented false starts.

An interesting sidelight on your own course of life can be found if you compare your chronology with that of the parent of your sex. Many of your life-expectations come from the model provided for you by that parent. Although it will not show up on any developmental scheme, the age at which a parent dies (especially if it is early) is likely to be an important point in your own life history. So can the point at which a parent's life comes together to become interesting and productive, or the point at which things seem to fall apart or go dead. What about the point at which your parent developed a serious illness or the point at which your parents divorced or the time that a parent changed the course of his or her life?

Comparing your chronology with that of your parents,

54

you are likely to discover milestones and detour markers that you scarcely noticed before. One of the men in the transition class discovered somewhat unexpectedly that he had quit his job at approximately the same age that his father had made a similar change twenty-five years earlier. "Am I copying him?" he asked, puzzled. "I hope not, because that decision was a terrible mistake for my father—he never found a really good job again after that." Another member of the class found close parallels between changes in her health and those of her mother, changes that had made a great impression on her as a girl. Still another class member had refused to retire at the usual time, not because he liked his work or because he needed the salary, but because his father had been miserable from the moment he retired.

It is important to identify those transition points that simply correspond to transitions that your parents made, since these points may well have nothing to do with the realities in your own life. In the same way, it is important to clarify how much of your experience in any transition time is actually yours and how much is a cultural overlay—fifty-year-olds are supposed to feel thus-and-so. Even the current theories about adult life can become a substitute for a real awareness of what is actually happening to you. For ultimately each of us is on a unique journey with a ticket marked "Good for this trip only—no transfers."

In spite of that fact, there are developmental issues that all of us deal with at some point along the way. The sphinx's riddle suggests the two most important ones—the transition process by which a dependent creature moves out into separate independence and develops a self-image and personal style that makes that possible. And then later, there is the point at which that same self-image and style hinders growth, and the person must go through the long, slow process of growing beyond them. Much of this later growth looks like loss, just as much of the earlier growth looks like gain. But that is no more true than the sense that spring is a season of gain and fall a season of loss. In fact each is essential to the full cycle, and the cycle is the only context in which the specific changes along the way have any real meaning.

3

LOVE AND
WORK

Freud was once asked what he thought a normal person should be able to do well. The questioner probably expected a complicated, "deep" answer. But Freud simply said, "Lieben und arbeiten" (to love and to work). It pays to ponder on this simple formula; it grows deeper as you think about it.

ERIK ERIKSON
Identity, Youth and Crisis[1]

Love relationships and work are the two most important factors through which a person's inner changes become visible. The first serious love of a person's life and the first long-term job are important turning points and are usually recognized as such. Each represents a new cluster of roles that the person is now ready to explore. As we have seen, many people make important commitments to another person or to a career during the novice period of adulthood as part of the larger task of searching for a place in the world. But that task soon gives way to others, and the individual continues an inner sequence of natural developmental transitions. How do these transitions affect the love-life and the work-life?

Their impact is enormous, for we are no longer talking about the individual in a social vacuum. In the case of a relationship, we are talking about the way in which the developmental rhythms of two people conflict and the way in which each of them may be influenced by changes in the relationship itself. "The end of the honeymoon," "the seven-year itch," and "the empty nest" all refer to a common awareness that relationships go through a logical sequence of changes and that these situations have an impact on the participants.

Even more complex are the effects that personal transitions have on one's work-life. The phase of life we move into or beyond—our morning, afternoon or evening—is greatly affected by the realities of our organizational or professional role. Even the course of personal growth is channeled by the somewhat prescribed routes of career advancement.

And yet when all this has been said, we also know that we tend to discover opportunities for change when we are ready. We say that we *have* to do the things that we do at home or at work, but that is only half true. When the man at the cocktail party tells us that he would like nothing better than to leave the big corporation and start his own business or to end a long-stalemated relationship, we commiserate because we know about responsibilities and commitments. But we also know that across the room stands someone who just did what this man "can't" do. Or isn't quite ready to do—which is nearer the truth.

Since *love* and *work* are such basic activities and so vital to our sense of well-being, we need to know more about how they affect and are affected by the transitions in our lives. When someone speaks of being in transition, the odds are that things are changing at home or at work. In some cases these changes are causes of personal transition, while in others they are the effects. Let us examine some of these changes in detail.

Personal transition and its impact on relationships

Let's begin with a family. Don, aged forty-one, is a teacher at the local high school; he's been there for twelve years and is getting bored with the place, with teaching, with teenagers—even with himself. Betty, aged thirty-nine, was a teacher, too, before the children were born, but she hasn't done anything much outside the home for fifteen years; now, however, she is talking about beginning a new career and going back to school to get a counseling license. Susan, aged sixteen, is a high school junior who is beginning to think about college; very bright and socially active, she is so busy that she sometimes seems to come home only to change clothes and to sleep. Bob, aged fifteen, is equally bright but much shyer and less busy; a whiz at math and science, he sometimes talks about a career in electrical engineering or aircraft design.

The stereotypical "happy family" in many ways, especially when they are portrayed in this snapshot fashion. But they are really people in motion, and the still picture cannot show this. Don, for example, is really distressed with his life these days. Sometimes, when the problem seems to be just the job, he thinks that if he finds something more interesting to do, everything will be better. But at other times he doubts that the answer can be so simple. He and Betty are arguing more than they ever have before—about her plans and their impact on the family, about his moodiness and lack of interest in anything. "I need a change. That's all," he says. But it sounds hollow, even to him.

In fact, his whole life has come to a standstill. He feels empty and lost. He looks at Betty across the table or the bedcovers and tries to remember the old attraction he felt for her. A nice person, certainly; quick and warm. How can he *not* find her attractive? Other men do. He noticed that at the party the other night. Not that she was leading them on—just that all evening she was talking to men, and he could see that they found her attractive. So why didn't he?

After the party they had come home and made love. Still excited by the evening, Betty was alive and responsive, and that turned him on. But only initially. After a little while, he lost his erection and they had to stop. This made Betty angry, and she wanted to know what was wrong. Nothing, nothing was wrong. This made her angrier, and she said harsh things about his being distant and cold. "You never used to be like this," she said. "What's happening to you?"

Don fought back, of course, but later, lying awake long after Betty had fallen asleep, her words echoed in his head. She was right. He never used to be like this. He thought of Pete, his lawyer and good friend, who had just left his family and moved into a city apartment. *He* had been bored, too. *He* had had trouble with sex, too. And now *he* had a whole new life, including fantastic sex again—at least, that's what he said. Maybe marriages have only so much shelf life—maybe they're only made to go 100,000 miles, maybe you're supposed to get a new one every fifteen years. Perhaps this was just the natural ending and it was only fear and guilt that held Don in place.

Dilemmas like these can plague younger couples, too. In fact there had been such dilemmas in Don and Betty's marriage ten or twelve years earlier, but at that time things hadn't seemed so serious. They had been married for five or six years, the kids were very young, and Don was just about to move to his present job. He remembered feeling dissatisfied then, too. Betty had not been very responsive sexually and they never seemed to go anywhere or do anything interesting. But the job at the new school had come to his rescue; Betty and the kids liked the new house, and everything seemed to have blown over. They were so busy and involved that their underlying responses to their transitions were never articulated. But now . . . would it blow over again?

That wasn't a question that could be easily answered because it depended not only on Don but on Betty and what she wanted out of life. When they moved into their house she had been tied down by two little children. "The only other adults I see all day," she used to say to Don, "are other trapped mothers, retired people, and the clerks at the Safeway. *You* get to see the world." Although she often was unhappy then, she saw no alternative. And worse, she suspected that if she thrashed around too much, Don, who was acting restless himself, would look for someone less bitchy and difficult.

But now things were different. Not that she wanted to leave the marriage—just that she no longer felt trapped in the old way. The children were almost on their own, and she had her new dream of a counseling career. She no longer had to accept an impossible situation. The long and lonely years of early parenthood were behind her, and she felt a new excitement at the thought of moving out and finding a separate place for herself in the world.

Yet the situation scared her too, for the better she felt about herself, the worse Don seemed to feel about himself. It was almost as though there were only enough energy for one, and the more she got, the less he got. His loss of interest in sex was an example. The other night was the worst, but it had been heading in that direction for some time. He always used to take the initiative sexually, often urging her to try things that she felt shy about trying or wanting to have sex when she really wasn't very interested. But now it was she, more often than not, who took the initiative. And it was she who seemed to enjoy sex more than he did. She was now more interested in sex and more responsive than she had been at thirty. She and Don were both changing, but changing, it seemed, in opposite directions. In time, she could imagine, they would have moved so far apart that they would be out of sight of each other.

It might be better if they separated. Maybe they had come to be bad for each other. Certainly he was a drain on her energy and he often felt like a dead weight that she had to lug around—like the other night at the party. Out of the corner of her eye, she saw him looking at her all night long as she talked and laughed with others. It was worse when she talked with men and felt enlivened by this interest in her. That was fun, and she had to admit that it made her realize that if she ever did leave Don she needn't resign herself to isolation and celibacy.

But the sexual thing was really secondary, she thought. The primary thing was her new sense of purpose and the readiness she felt to meet the world head-on. She was ready to *do* things, and she hadn't felt that way since she graduated from college. The only problem was, could she keep feeling this way around Don? Would she have to choose between checking her own momentum and leaving him behind? She could suggest that he see a psychotherapist, but he would just say, "That's your old counselor number again, Betty. I'll handle this my way." Would this all just blow over, or was she going to have to do something?

That question hinges on what is meant by "blow over." If one means the particulars—the fight last night and today's tensions—then the answer may well be *yes*. The old ups and downs are replaced by new ups and downs. But if one means the changes going on within these two individuals and the transition that their relationship is consequently going through, then the answer is probably *no*. For those changes are deep and far-reaching.

What is happening to each of these individuals is that they are coming to a point of separate, personal transition that is having an impact on their marriage. In coming to the end of a phase of their lives they are finding that the marriage that served them more or less well up to this point is being put under enormous strain. The sexual difficulties are just the tip of the iceberg, and a repair job there will simply transfer the difficulty to some new area. Communication is terribly important, but it is finding out what they really want to say to each other that is crucial. And, yes, roles need to be renegotiated, too, but not until these two people can go through their transitions can any enduring arrangement be devised.

You have probably already realized that neither Don nor Betty gave themselves room to deal with any second thoughts that may have first surfaced ten years earlier. They felt that they couldn't afford to, and a new external situation came along to distract them. In fact, Don had been unhappy with teaching then and had begun to realize that he had originally seized on that kind of work because he had always liked school and didn't know what else to do. But the new job, together with a new home in a new community, made him forget his doubts and his longing for a deeper kind of new beginning.

It had also been so with Betty. The product of a very traditional upbringing, she had never really asked herself whether she wanted children right away. In spite of having just taken a job, she got pregnant and "had to" leave her career.

Neither Betty nor Don had changed much between the ages of twenty and thirty-five, but from that point on both of them found it more and more difficult to summon up the energy necessary to do the old things in the old way. But their situations were different. Betty had the built-in ending of the children's independence. As they got older, they needed her less and less, and her original motivation toward a career was awakened.

But Don had no built-in ending—not, at least, until retirement, and he certainly couldn't wait that long for relief. Nor was leaving teaching really the issue at this point, for the onerous responsibility of work that he did not like was only a symptom of a deeper difficulty. Having been a stranger to his own real needs and interests for so long, he no longer knew what he wanted or even who he was. "I feel that I left myself a thousand miles back, somewhere," he said later when he and Betty came in for counseling. "The train just went on and on until finally it ran out of fuel and stopped, and then I couldn't pretend any longer that everything was OK."

Don's *problem*—whether you take that to be impotence or boredom with work or loss of interest in marriage—was not the important thing, and any attempt to deal with the problem in a mechanical way would have provided no solution. It would have been like fueling up the train again and sending it further down the track into the wilderness. The *problem* was in fact a signal that the time had come to stop something—but not to stop teaching or to end the marriage or to cease making love, but rather to recognize "the end of the line" when it came.

In Don's case this recognition led to far-reaching changes over the next several years. After the first impulses to leave his career and his marriage, he decided to stay with both. He and Betty worked out a time plan for the next two years, at which time she would be working and earning enough money to take some of the pressure off Don. Meanwhile, he began a systematic survey of his own experience to see what kinds of things he really liked to do. For a while this produced a new source of conflict. While he was sure that a life of thoughtful inactivity by some modern-day Walden Pond was his answer, she was equally sure that she could never be happy without friends. ("I had my Walden," she said, "alone at home when the children were little.")

That storm passed, though, and they both kept working to find just what it was that they really wanted, alone and together. While an answer was slow in taking shape, both of them felt a great sense of relief in having acknowledged that the old way was no longer viable and that they were, in fact, in transition.

The new beginning, when it did finally emerge, seemed almost ridiculously easy in comparison to the great effort that they had devoted to finding it. One day Don bumped into an old school friend whose father, a small-town newspaper editor in another part of the state, had just died. The friend had to sell the paper as soon as possible and he asked Don, who was the adviser to the school newspaper, if he by any chance knew anyone who was looking for a small but successful weekly.

Before deciding to buy the paper, Don and Betty checked out the town with an eye to Betty's career. "If I'd gone along just for Don's sake, we'd have been back in our old pattern again," Betty explained later. "But it turned out fine. I got a job with the county mental health agency, and it is a perfect place to get the supervision I need for my license. We have a different kind of marriage now, and the transition wasn't easy. But both of us are happy, and we're learning things about ourselves and each other every day. If we'd started over again with two new partners, it would have been a replay, I expect. But as it is, we're out on the frontier of our lives, exploring new territory."

Transition, relationships, and resonance

We'll come back to Don and Betty again when we talk about the transition process in detail and refer to their experiences in ending, exploring the nowhere between the old and the new, and beginning anew. But there is another aspect of their family life that involves transition and needs to be noted here. That is the phenomemon of "resonance" or the way in which the developmental issues being dealt with by one member of a family awaken or intensify similar issues in another, in the same way that one string can set another vibrating when it is plucked.

Don and Betty had two teenagers, and each of the children was in the midst of that extended transition toward personal independence. At fifteen and sixteen, they were volatile: full of enthusiasm one day and ready to chuck everything the next. Bob exhausted new careers on a daily basis; first he was going to be a test pilot, then an atomic physicist, then a computer engineer, then . . . . Meanwhile, he was slow to mature socially and didn't date at all.

Don found his son both easy to understand and strangely frustrating. Bob reminded his father of himself at fifteen—a crazy mixture of confidence and self-doubt—and Don sympathized with his son's confusions about himself. At the same time, Don found himself unexpectedly invested in Bob's career dreams. "I see him, so bright and capable in science and so interested in things I never dreamed of at his age, and I think, 'Go for it, kid! Don't take the safe route and be sorry later—the way I've been.' "

At first Don chalked these reactions up to "normal parental concern" for his son's future welfare, but in time he began to think something more was involved. "Here I am, stalled and lost at this transition point in my life, and I can hardly stand to watch my son as he teeters back and forth on the edge of a big step in his life. When he applied to Cal Tech, I felt a sense of relief. It was more than pride, although I felt that too, of course. It was as though Bob was finally going to make something of himself and in so doing, make something of me too. He was my proxy, sent out to the world to do the business that I hadn't been able to finish. But when I realized that, I decided, 'Hey, this isn't good for either of us. He can't do it for you, and your investment in him that way will just be a burden to him.' So I backed off."

This resonance between a child and a parent is common when the two of them arrive at transition points at the same time. Betty found the same thing happening to her when her daughter was going off to college. "I think that you're more excited by my departure than I am," Susan remarked to her mother one day. "It feels like you're trying to get rid of me."

In explaining that she did not feel that way, Betty discovered that the charge behind her reaction came from the same kind of proxy-granting that Don discovered with Bob. "She's heading out on her own," Betty said, in describing this discovery, "and her freedom stirs something very deep in me. I never gave myself that freedom, and I don't know that I really want it now. But I have to say that it really excites me."

Susan's freedom at this time included exploring her sexuality in several different relationships. This alternately disturbed and amazed her mother. "Wouldn't you know that she'd be doing that just at the same time I'm reevaluating my marriage and aware that I'm still attractive to men and that Don's turned off sexually!" It would have been easy, Betty realized, to transfer her own longings to her daughter. "I could stay faithful and live out my desires vicariously," she said with a little laugh. "But I guess it'll be better if I do my own business and let her do hers."

Transition and the interpersonal system

Families, like organizations and interpersonal groupings of all kinds, are "systems." That is the members are not autonomous entities that happen to be together, but are actually parts of a larger whole and are affected by anything that happens to that whole. Furthermore, it is characteristic of all systems that although their members may consciously try to change the parts that they or others play in the system, the members also often unwittingly perpetuate the system in its current form by undermining attempts to change it.

A case in point. Both Don and Betty wanted their kids to launch out into the world, and each parent had a special reason to be interested—Don through his thwarted career dreams and Betty through her longing for freedom. Yet both of them also were scared of their kids' transitions. "As long as they're at home, we're a *family,* and Don and I have something important to do together, which is to parent the kids." Betty certainly didn't want to stand in the way of her kids, but at this time of transition in her marriage she felt very vulnerable. "If we aren't parents, what are we?" she asked Don on one occasion.

Many parents are far less aware of this resistance to change. "He's still a little boy to us," they say innocently of the thirty-year-old lawyer son. "She's not good enough for you," they say of the "girl" (who is, after all, thirty herself) that he is going out with. "Blood is thicker than water, son" (meaning, "nothing will ever replace your ties to us").

These reactions are not limited to parents whose children are leaving the nest. Any time that any member of a system changes, the other members will feel a twinge. Children are bothered when divorced or widowed parents begin to date again. Siblings conspire to keep one another in line, long after they have stopped living under the same roof. And, of course, partners in any intimate relationship react with alarm to unexpected changes in the other person.

Nothing makes it clearer how a relationship is structured with complementary roles than this reaction to the other person's transition. A husband may be aware of feeling only supportive or even pleased at some important new beginning in his wife's life, but will later discover himself to be undermining it unwittingly. ("Really, I'm *thrilled* that you are going back to graduate school—I don't know why I forgot my promise to cook dinner . . . pick up the kids . . . straighten out the house before you came home.") It is as though the wife has violated some unspoken rule by being in transition.

Well, she has. Although people are seldom conscious of the fact, relationships are always structured by unspoken agreements. Beginning very early in the relationship, there is a psychological division of labor: One person takes care of the practical issues and the other handles the human ones; or one expresses emotions and the other anchors the relationship; or one is full of plans and the other is the tough critic. Each has always been somewhat that way, but the partnership lets them become more so—until one person becomes a stand-in for the undeveloped side of the other's personality.

Then the controlled and rational one discovers that life involves more than bookkeeping and contracts. Panic! The Rock of Gibraltar is crumbling! The other's world begins to come apart, since Old-Cool-and-Steady's transition leaves one whole flank exposed on his mate. The same thing happens if Sensitive-and-Warm begins to have ideas of her own about where she's headed and how to get there. Panic! The light of life is going out. Her spouse's whole world sputters and slows down, threatening to get stuck in some lonely byway.

This panic at a spouse's change is natural. It's like the anxiety that an actor would feel when his cue produces no entrance and no response. Or worse yet, some response that isn't in the script. ("My God! She said *no*. She was supposed to say *yes.* How do I reply, and where does our drama go from here?")

Why is this? Are we so reactionary as creatures that we do not change except when someone else forces us to? Are we like pool balls, sitting forever in a fixed pattern until some interpersonal cueball blasts us into motion? I think not, although we do have a kind of inner inertia when circumstances initiate transition. But it is not as mechanical as the table full of pool balls. Rather, we are more like stories that are slowly unfolding according to our own inner theme and plot. Each person's life is a story that is telling itself in the living, and each requires others to play certain kinds of roles. (Wanted: A warm, unassertive woman to soothe a middle-aged and rapidly tiring knight on a decrepit horse.) Each of us resists change because a story is a self-coherent world with its own kind of immune system. Alien characters are out of place. (Think of trying to fit Dick Tracy into *Hamlet,* or Lady Chatterly into *Little House on the Prairie.*)

To become a couple is to agree implicitly to live in terms of another person's story, although it sometimes takes time to get the part down really well. It isn't enough to follow the overt signals, for the part is often that of one who "never does what is asked." An outsider listening to the dialogue would probably misunderstand the agreement between the two people. "He's urging you to go out and get a job," the outsider may say. "Why don't you do it?" Whatever the wife may reply, she knows deep in her bones that it is not so simple—that her husband is really saying something like, "You poor, timid soul. You can't really face the world, can you? But that's all right because I'll take care of you."

This is all hidden from view, of course—or it is until one day the wife comes home and says, with her heart in her throat, "Guess what. I got a job." And he says, "You *did?*" And he looks at her strangely or says rather unconvincingly, "That's wonderful." In a few minutes, he'll say unexpectedly, "Well, who the hell is going to pick up the stuff at the cleaners, then?"

A couple can find lots of help on how they ought to be: less sexist, say, or more open in their communication, or more accepting of each other. But they will have a far harder time finding help with the issue of how to change or how to let their partner change within a relationship. This is unfortunate because in such a situation what is at stake is not only the relationship but also the on-going development of each partner.

In the next three chapters we will be looking at some of the strategies for dealing constructively with change, but it is important to note here the real developmental issue involving relationships in transition. Whatever the current antagonisms and topics that a couple is trying to deal with, a life transition brings them to the point where each has the opportunity to discover the inner resources that have hitherto been expressed in the relationship through the other person. Each has the opportunity to be more whole, more complete as a person. The relationship can then be renegotiated on a less restrictive basis.

This process of renegotiation must take place many times during a long-term relationship if it is to stay vital and provide both partners with a setting for their continued development. The process often goes on unconsciously as each person deals with the other's transitions—and with the changing lives of any children they may have. It isn't necessarily a self-conscious procedure, like the arbitration of a labor dispute. It is simply the reorganization of the domestic system whenever an ending point is reached. And the process is greatly facilitated by the recognition that a relationship, like the lives that come together in it, has its seasons and its times of turning. Problems, in that view, are often the signals for the ending of a chapter.

When a couple can share this awareness and explore its significance in their present situation, they can transform a threatening difficulty into an opportunity. If you cannot get your partner to join you in this view and this exploration, however, you will need to begin alone. Of course, the great temptation is to pour your energy into trying to make your partner see things differently. I frequently get visits from husbands or wives who announce that a spouse is "in a mid-life crisis" or at some other transition point and needs to be talked to. "He'll listen to you. He really needs help."

That may be so, of course, but it simply won't work to provide help that is not wanted at that point. What does work is for the partner who is aware of the transition process and its implications for a relationship to begin exploring alone the question of what is ending in the relationship and what to do about it. More often than not, it turns out that what is ending is not some external situation but an attitude or an assumption or a self-image. And the husbands or wives who began by being sure that the partner needed help find that the need is within themselves, and that once the inner change is made, the other person proves to be not nearly so blind or unwilling to talk as it had previously seemed. I have come to regard it as a rule of thumb that husbands or wives seeking help and advice for a spouse had better face their own need for help.

Transitions in the work-life

Many of the things said about the effects of transition within the family system are equally true in regard to the work-place. Any person who is in transition sets up patterns of resonance at work as well as at home. I remember encountering this difficulty myself when I was getting ready to leave a teaching career. Although I knew little about life-transitions then, I had a sense that I needed some free space between my old work and my new, whatever that work might turn out to be. I therefore set things up so that I could get by for some months with only short-term work.

When I told the members of my department about this plan, one of them said, "But where are you going to teach?" I explained that I wasn't going to teach anywhere for a while, so that I could get a fresh perspective on my work-life. He looked dismayed but said nothing. A week later I bumped into him in the faculty dining room where he was eating with another friend. "I was just telling Bob about your leaving the college," he said when I joined them, "but I couldn't remember where you said you were going to teach." When I reminded him that I was not going to teach anywhere, he denied having heard that before. "Not teach anywhere!" he said, surprised. "That's a big step."

I was confused at his reaction and wondered if I had imagined our earlier conversation. Then a week later he cleared up the confusion by "forgetting" again and being amazed for the third time by the news that I was really leaving teaching. He was a man who was quite unhappy with his work, but several years earlier he had decided that he was too old to make a career shift. The work-place is full of such people—and all of them have their own reasons for resonating to another individual's retirement, transfer, promotion, or firing.

A person's career, like a long-term relationship, goes through a sequence of phases. To begin a new job is to encounter the same kinds of difficulties that one finds in beginning a new relationship. There is a period of adjustment in each case, although "adjustment" is a misleadingly mechanistic concept. It suggests that you need to fiddle with the dials and reset the switches to adapt yourself to the new situation. The trouble with this view is that although there are difficult changes to be made as one gets used to a new situation, the difficulty comes not from these changes but from the larger process of letting go of the person you used to be and then finding the new person you have become in the new situation. The real difficulties, in short, come from the transition process.

It is important to understand the centrality of this process in many work- and career-related changes. Getting fired feels very different from changing a job intentionally, and both situations seem quite different from those mysterious doldrums that turn previously interesting jobs into purgatories. And all of these seem different from taking a first job, or retiring, or getting transferred. But under the surface of all of them is the experience of transition, and it is that experience that brings about the distress rather than the problem of adjusting to the new situation. In the next chapters we will discuss in detail the three phases of the transition process and how to deal constructively with them. Here we will concentrate on how personal transition affects the work-life.

Regardless of what is changing in a person's life—marital status, health, finances or spiritual beliefs—work is affected. Sometimes the change intensifies a person's energy, but more often it diverts energy from work to that area of the person's life that is changing. "I don't know what's happening to Shirley [or Charley]," a supervisor may say in puzzlement. "She [or he] used to be such a hard worker, but lately. . . ."

What's happening is, of course, the whole transition process, but a supervisor, seeing only the changes in motivation, will probably try to reactivate the old motivation by threats or by a raise or by a change in job assignment. This remedy misses the point, for what is happening is not that the person is simply losing interest (which might indeed be restimulated) or getting tired of the same old stuff (in which case, a change might renew interest). What is happening is that in ending and letting go of what he or she has been—which often marks the beginning of the transition process—a person loses the old connections to the activities and the people that used to matter. In the turning cycle of change, this is the *fall* and any attempts to reinstate the old motivations by reward and punishment are as futile as an attempt to keep the leaves on the trees.

To understand better what this actually means as well as what can be done about it, let's return to the case of Don. None of his co-workers had any clear sense of what was going on in his life, but it was obvious to everyone that Don was doing a halfhearted job of teaching. When his principal talked to him about it, Don promised to try harder and left the confrontation feeling scared and confused.

Part of his confusion came from the gradual recognition that it wasn't just that home issues were undermining him at work; it was that *the same issues that were undermining him as a teacher were undermining him as a husband and a father*. In all areas of his life he felt a sense of emptiness and meaninglessness.

Don had unearthed a significant truth about his situation and over the ensuing months he thought about it a great deal. In the process, he discovered one of the important transitions that is likely to take place in a person's work-life: the transition from being motivated by the chance to demonstrate competence to being motivated by the chance to find meaning. It is the shift from the question of *how* to the question of *why*.

The work world knows all about competence. Most evaluations and rewards are determined by a person's competence. Vocational guidance emphasizes it in testing which areas of work one would be most competent in. Transfers and promotions are based on competence. In business and the professions, you get in and get ahead by demonstrating your competence.

But somewhere along the way—as early as thirty-five for some and as late as fifty-five for others—competence begins to lose its force as a source of motivation. The doctor says, "Yes, I'm a good surgeon, but the technical challenges just don't interest me as they used to. What's the point of doing the same things over and over again?" And the plumber and the social worker and the house-keeper say the same thing. Of course, the old flame can be rekindled temporarily by shifting to a new area where you must begin all over again and develop new competence, but the effects are usually short-lived. The season of competence is passing, in spite of some late-flowering trans-plants.

For months Don wrestled with the question of what he wanted. Bit by bit it came clear. Having spent most of his working life with ideas and theory, he longed to do some-thing that involved practical action. He liked writing, but he didn't have any books waiting to be born. And then he heard about the newspaper that was for sale.

It was a slow process, as most life transitions are. It meant working out ways of living with the transition pro-cess over a period of months or even years. Don did it by holding on to his old job while he found what he wanted to do next. This was difficult because he was, as he said, "emotionally unplugged" from what he was doing. But having made sense out of that experience he stopped fighting it. He found it tolerable and transferred his real energy to the larger undertaking of finding a new direction for himself.

Not everyone can make a vocational transition this way. If Don had been fired, he would have had to find a new job to support him while he went through his transition. Perhaps the pressure to find the new job would have accelerated the process a little, although transition seems to have a timing of its own and a way of resisting efforts to rush it. If Don had been at some other point in his life, his transition would have involved different issues entirely.

The work-life, like the love-life, has its own natural rhythm. The task is to find the relation between the actual change in work or career and the underlying developmental rhythm. The books on adulthood offer some clues, but everyone's life history is unique. There is no litmus paper that will turn pink or blue to test the life situation, and the task of finding the significance of a particular transition may be slow and difficult. Unless that significance is found, however, the thread of personal development will be lost and one will be left with an inexplicable change and an overwhelming desire to put the pieces back together again as quickly as possible.

Although there are no ways to tell you what a particular change means, there are ways of maximizing your chances of finding that meaning and they apply equally to the world of relationships and to the world of work. We will end the chapter by listing them in the form of a checklist.

Love and work: a transition checklist

1. *Take your time.* The outer forms of our lives can change in an instant, but the inner reorientation that brings us back into a vital relation to people and activity takes time. This does not mean that everything must come to a total standstill while you wait for self-renewal. But it does mean that your commitments, either to the old situation that you haven't yet left or the new situation that you haven't yet invested yourself in, are going to be somewhat

provisional. And it means that you cannot rush the inner process whereby this state of affairs will change.

2. *Arrange temporary structures.* When we had our house remodeled a few years ago, we tolerated for several weeks a living room wall made of plastic and canvas. That temporary construction was ugly, but it provided us with the protection we needed to go on living in a space that was being transformed. So it is with transitional situations in love and work: you will need to work out ways of going on while the inner work is being done. This may involve getting a temporary job while you look for a real job; it may involve agreements at home or at work to carry on in some modified fashion until something more permanent can be devised; or it may simply involve an inner resolve to accept a given situation as temporary and to transfer some energy to the job of finding a replacement for it.

3. *Don't act for the sake of action.* The temporary situation is frustrating and there is likely to be a temptation to "do something—anything." This reaction is understandable, but it usually leads to more difficulty. The transition process requires not only that we bring a chapter of our lives to conclusion, but that we discover whatever we need to learn for the next step we are going to take. We need to stay in transition long enough to complete this important process, not to abort it through premature action.

4. *Recognize why you are uncomfortable.* Distress is not a sign that something has gone wrong but that something is changing. Understanding the transition process, expecting times of anxiety, expecting others to be threatened, expecting old fears to be awakened—all of these things are very important. Read over the second half of this book carefully and use the model of personal transition provided there to make sense out of the confusions and pain that you may be experiencing.

5. *Take care of yourself in little ways.* This is probably not the time to be living up to your highest self-image, although it is a time to keep your agreements carefully. Be sensitive to your smallest needs and don't force change on yourself as though it were medicine. Find the little continuities that are important when everything else seems to be changing. A friend of mine took her elderly mother to the supermarket the day after she had moved to a new house and a new town. "Bananas, we've got to get bananas for your father," her mother said. It was the wrong time of year and bananas were expensive, but in a situation where everything else in their lives had changed, it was important to hold on to a few continuities, like favorite foods or a schedule of familiar TV programs.

6. *Explore the other side of the change.* Some changes are chosen and some are not, and each kind of transition has its own difficulties. If you have not chosen a change, there are a dozen reasons to refuse to see its possible benefits—for by seeing such benefits you may undercut your anger at whoever forced the change on you, or you may realize that the old situation wasn't all that you thought it was. On the other hand, if you have chosen your change, there are just as many reasons not to want to consider the cost—for that may weaken your resolve, or make you aware of the pain your transition brings to others. In either case, you will need to explore the other side of the situation.

7. *Get someone to talk to.* Whether you choose a professional counselor or just a good friend, you will need someone to talk to when you are going through an important transition in your work-life or your relationships. What you primarily need is not advice, although that may occasionally be useful, but rather to put into words your dilemmas and your feelings so that you can fully understand what is going on. Beware of the listener who "knows exactly what you ought to do," but also be suspicious if you

find yourself explaining away your listener's reactions if they don't happen to fit with yours—especially if several people have reacted the same way to what you say.

8. *Find out what is waiting in the wings of your life.* Whether you chose your change or not, there are unlived potentialities within you, interests and talents that you have not yet explored. Transitions clear the ground for new growth. They drop the curtain so that the stage can be set for a new scene. What is it, at this point in your life, that is waiting quietly backstage for an entrance cue? What new growth is ready to germinate in this season of your life? These are questions that you can talk about with a confidant, or you can privately explore them in writing in a transition journal. You could get a piece of paper right now and write at the top, "What Is Waiting to Happen in My Life Now," and begin writing. (Don't plan it out or try to figure out the answer in advance; just start writing and write as quickly as you can. You will be surprised what comes out once you have given up deciding in advance what you are going to say.)

9. *Use this transition as the impetus to a new kind of learning.* You knew much of what you needed to know for what you were, but what you are going to become will require new understandings and new skills that you may not yet possess. Edward Gibbon wrote that "every man who rises above the common level has received two educations: the first from his teachers; the second, more personal and important, from himself." This transition point in your life may well be the time to launch that second education—or to begin it again, for while the first education follows a fixed curriculum to a stopping point, the second education opens out into new areas at every turning point.

10. *Recognize that transition has a characteristic shape.* Arnold Toynbee pointed out years ago in *The Study of History* that societies gain access to new energies and

new directions only after a "time of troubles" initiates a process of disintegration wherein the old order comes apart; and he showed how often the new orientation is made clear only after what he calls a "withdrawal and return" on the part of individuals or creative minorities within the society. The crucial change, it seems, takes place in some in-between state or outside the margin of ordinary life. That is so with individual lives as well: Things end, there is a time of fertile emptiness, and then things begin anew. And it is to that characteristic sequence that we must now turn.

PART TWO

THE
TRANSITION
PROCESS

Initiation is so closely linked to the
mode of being of human existence
that a considerable number of
modern man's acts and gestures
continue to repeat initiatory
scenarios. Very often the "struggle
for life," the "ordeals" and
"difficulties" that stand in the way of
a vocation or a career in some sort
reiterate the ordeals of initiation.

MIRCEA ELIADE
The Sacred and The Profane[1]

His face and body are whitened with clay, and he is no
longer recognizable as the youth who left his village two
months before. The wounds of his ordeal—a circumcision
and the parallel scars across his cheeks—are healed now.
But they will always bear witness to what he has suffered.
They mark him as one who has crossed the boundary of
childhood and has put that life behind him.

He is alone. More than simply out of contact with his
peers and his elders, he is absolutely and radically alone.
In this time (or time-out) of his life, he is out of relation
with all others. In space, too, he is beyond the edge of his
old world. There is no map on which one could point and
say, "There he is." There is no *there* there, since he in-
habits for this time a non-place.

He is beyond the mediating power of roles and relationships and social mores. Armed only with the rituals
and chants taught him by an initiation master, he wan-
ders free and unattached through the universe. Beyond
the meaning-making powers of his everyday realities, he
stands face to face with existence.

At night he dreams, and the dreams of this primal

non-time and non-place are full of enigmatic hints and presences. Each night he goes to sleep praying that this will be the night of the great vision. It will be then and thus that he discovers his spirit guide or his guardian elder. That voice will tell him of his true vocation and his real name. It may teach him a sacred chant to heal the sick or to bless the newly-planted corn.

When this has happened, he will know that it is time to return to the village and take up the rights and responsibilities of his new status and his new identity. Marked by his scars and empowered by his new knowledge, he will rejoin the social order on a new basis. He is in a profound sense a new person.

The one that he used to be is dead. It died in the ordeal and the mortuary ritual with which his rite of passage began. His parents signified this death by burning the sleeping mat that he had used all through childhood. When he returns to the village, he will not recognize them—at least at first. For he is no longer theirs.

In the first weeks of his new life back in the village, he will not remember his old name. He is reborn, and for a time his behavior will recall that of a very small child again. He will have forgotten how to do very basic things—washing and feeding himself, for example. He will be unable to remember the old terms for familiar objects, although from his time with the initiation master he has strange new names for many of these objects. To some degree and on some occasions, he actually speaks a new language.

The youth has been renewed and enlightened by his ritual transition. The time-out in the non-place was his gateway to the original chaos from which the gods fashioned the world in the beginning. All new form, his people believed, must begin in that chaos, and any gap in time or space may provide access to it. Such gaps occur at the end of any cycle. At the end of a year or a season, at the end of the reign of a chief, and at the end of any phase in the individual's own life, nature or the society or the person enters the gap and dies. After a time each is reborn, and that is the way in which life sustains itself. It is the way of withdrawal and return. It is the way of forgetting and rediscovery. It is the way of ending and beginning. In following it, the person crosses over from an old way of being to a new way of being and is renewed in the process.

This description of a youth in the midst of a rite of passage is a composite one.[2] In one tribe a tooth would have been knocked out, but there would have been no scars. In another place, it would have been a group of initiates rather than an individual that would have been isolated in the wilderness beyond the known village world. In some cultures the initiation master or the elders would have planted the seeds of new understanding in the fertile ground of the gap, rather than leaving it up to the initiate's own visions and intuitions. The details of the ritual would have changed greatly from place to place, but the process of passage would have remained the same.

It was Arnold van Gennep, a Dutch anthropologist, who first interpreted these rites for a modern, western audience almost seventy-five years ago. It was he who coined the term, *rites of passage*, and it was he who pointed out that such rites were the way in which traditional societies structured life transitions.[3] He grouped together rituals dealing with birth and death, with puberty and marriage, with the election of a chief and the creation of a shaman, with the person's entry into a secret society of men or women, and with nature's entry into a new season—and he saw that all of these ceremonial occasions were made up of three phases that he called *separation*, *transition*, and *incorporation*.

In the first phase the person or the group was separated from the old and familiar social context and was put through a symbolic death experience. Then came a time in isolation in what van Gennep called the "neutral zone," a no man's land between the old way of being and the new. Finally, when the intended inner changes had taken place, the person or group was brought back and reintegrated into the social order on a new basis. Although some rituals emphasized one phase and minimized another, all passage rites revealed this three-phase form to a remarkable extent.

Since van Gennep's time, a kind of nostalgia has built up around the notion of rites of passage. We moderns lack them, for the most part, and many people have remarked on this lack. Since we also have great difficulty with life transitions, some people think it logical that we could improve our situation by recreating ritualized transitions in our lives. But rites do not transplant well. They are not techniques for doing something but lenses through which to magnify the experience of something. Rituals of passage are simply a way of focusing and making more visible the natural pattern of dying, chaos, and renewal that was believed to operate everywhere in the universe. And without that belief, there is nothing to focus. Unless a culture and its members see life transitions in that way, the rituals will be rejected like a transplant from an alien organism.

So in its simple form, the nostalgia for rites of passage is misplaced. But the rituals are important to understand all the same. Developed in cultures that were extremely sensitive to the dynamics of personal transformation, passage rituals are our best records of the natural shape of personal change. Far less exposed to external changes than our own society is, these cultures were remarkably sophisticated in their understanding of the inner process of transition. Behind the strangeness of their surfaces, they can provide us with names for the elements of our own experience that are distressing and perplexing because they are otherwise nameless.

From here on we will follow the lead of these cultures by examining the three natural phases of transition. Named "Endings," "The Neutral Zone," and "The New Beginning," these aspects of personal change will be explored in detail so that you can understand why your own experience of transition takes the shape that it does, and how you can deal more constructively with it. For as the ancients knew, transition is the way of personal development.

4

ENDINGS

What we call the beginning is often the end
And to make an end is to make a beginning.
The end is where we start from.

T.S. ELIOT
"Little Gidding"[1]

Considering that we have to deal with endings all our lives, most of us handle them very badly. This is in part because we misunderstand them and take them either too seriously or not seriously enough. We take them too seriously by confusing them with finality—that's it, all over, never more, finished! We see them as something without sequel, forgetting that in fact they are the first phase of the transition process and a precondition of self-renewal. At the same time we fail to take them seriously enough. Just because they scare us, we try to avoid them.

"I don't want to talk about the past," says a newly married man who has come in to talk about his second marriage. "I'm interested in the present and the future." How can I make him understand that his so-called present is a past that he hasn't yet let go of? His wife tried to tell him that when she yelled that he was still emotionally tied to his first wife. "No, I'm interested in us," he said. "It just bothers me when you do things the way she did. I want things to be different." But he doesn't want to talk about the past.

I try a story with him. "Once there were two monks who were traveling through the countryside during the rainy season. Rounding a bend in the path, they found a muddy stream blocking their way. Beside it stood a lovely woman dressed in flowing robes. 'Here,' said one of the monks to the woman. 'Let me carry you across the water.'

And he picked her up and carried her across. Setting her down on the further bank, he went along in silence with his fellow monk to the abbey on the hill. Later that evening the other monk said suddenly, 'I think you made an error, picking up that woman back on our journey today. You know we are not supposed to have anything to do with women, and you held one close to you! You should not have done that.' 'How strange,' remarked the other. 'I carried her only across the water. You are carrying her still.[2]

I look at the man to see if he has understood, but he hasn't. He wants to talk about his new marriage and finds my questions about his old marriage irritating. He wants to get on with beginnings. The hell with endings!

We all know how the man feels, and yet endings must be dealt with if we are to move on to whatever comes next in our lives. The new growth cannot take root on ground still covered with the old, and endings are the clearing process. No longer ritualized and formally prepared for us, endings happen to us in unforeseeable ways that often seem devoid of any meaning—much less of any positive meaning. Instead they are simply events that we try to move beyond as quickly as possible. Even our language reflects this attitude: "Don't cry over spilt milk." "What's done is done." "Let bygones be bygones."

These attitudes were epitomized in that first transition class by the woman with the new baby who, objecting to our attention to endings, cracked, "I'm just trying to get used to having him, not sending him off to college." And her classmate who was getting used to the big promotion likewise found our concern for endings strange at first: "About all that I am giving up is low pay and low status," he said skeptically. But as we talked further, each of them discovered that the ending was not only real but important to understand and appreciate. For it wasn't the new beginning that accounted for the confusions that they were experiencing but rather the termination of the old life that they had previously led.

One of the advantages of being familiar with passage rituals is that they make it clear that the ending involves a symbolic death. When the new mother shouted "I am falling apart!" at the class, she was telling the truth—the "she" that she had hitherto identified with was disintegrating. Because of her view that disintegration meant malfunction, she assumed that what she needed was a way to repair her life; but she quickly came to see that no mere fixing up of things would suffice. All of that good advice she kept asking for was beside the point, for her real need then was to find out how to let the person-that-she-had-been die and go through a renewal process.

The old passage rituals are one answer, though they depend on a social reality and a mythic imagination that is rare today. All the same, they provide a way of understanding the natural ending process and provide suggestive parallels to our own unritualized experience. To show how this is so, I will discuss the four different aspects of the natural ending experience: disengagement, disidentification, disenchantment, and disorientation.

Disengagement

It seems to be a universal belief among traditional peoples that at times of inner transition a person needs to be separated from the familiar place in the social order. The young initiate is removed from his or her family, sometimes forcibly, and taken out into the forest or the desert. The prospective shaman leaves the village and goes on a long trek of self-discovery. The same thing happens at marriage and at other life transition points such as those of entering a secret society or the circle of the elders or finally death itself.

In stories of the ancient world, this step of disengagement is a frequent theme. Christ makes a forty-day journey into the wilderness; Theseus leaves the familiar world of Troetzen for the tests and ordeals of the overland journey to Athens. Sometimes in these stories the disengagement is undertaken unwittingly or with some other conscious intent, as though the everyday mind were unable to grasp the person's real need at such a time and so the person had to act *as if* he or she were not seeking disengagement. Jonah flees his vocation and heads to sea, but he believes that he is going to Tarshish. Oedipus leaves home to avoid a fate that as it turns out he meets along the way. Both Jonah and Oedipus find that the first step toward destiny is taken in what seems to be the opposite direction. And both find that, whatever the circumstances, there is a natural tendency to break with the familiar social matrix at times of life transition.

We no longer have oracles and visions—at least we usually assume that we do not. No initiation master rings the bell one morning and says, "Your time is come." But all the same, we do find ourselves periodically being disengaged either willingly or unwillingly from the activities, the relationships, the settings, or the roles that have been important to us. What if these often distressing losses were really symbolic events? What if they were signals that a time of personal transition was beginning?

To ask such questions when the loss is fresh is often a pointless exercise and may even be a cruel one. The person who has just been fired or lost a parent or had a heart attack is not in any frame of mind to listen to talk about symbolic events—and certainly not to hear that it may be "all for the best." But such people often come to such conclusions at some later point in the experience. Connie was a case in point.

93

She had originally come up after a lecture to say that her husband was showing all the signs of a mid-life crisis, whatever that was, and she wished that I would talk to him. He hadn't come to the lecture himself because he didn't think anything was wrong with him. "Hell no," he'd told her the night before. "I'm just catching on to what life is about, and I'm damned if I'm going to spend the rest of my life cutting along the dotted line!" In the few minutes that we talked, I gave my usual explanation of why it seldom does much good to try to help someone who doesn't want help—and I suggested that perhaps she might be able to use some help on the question of where *she* was in her life just now. She looked dismayed. Clearly, I wasn't going to be much help.

I saw her three or four months later, and everything had fallen apart. Her husband had suddenly left one evening and was now living in a nearby city. In the next couple of weeks there had been some dreadful fights on the telephone, then some dreary negotiations about money and about the children, and finally the start of divorce proceedings. "I can't pretend it's not all over now," Connie said sadly, "but I'd give anything if it weren't."

The main topics of our discussions in that first couple of months were practical—how to talk about the divorce to the kids, how to find work, how to deal with her parents, and how to start a social life again. Whenever the talk turned to the meaning of the separation, she'd say angrily, "You'll have to ask him. He was the one who did it."

In time, however, this changed. She began to talk about what she had lost. She had lost a great deal of security, for one thing, because all the family income came from her husband's work. She had lost companionship, for although he had traveled a good deal, she had never felt "alone in the world," as she put it. She had lost a sexual partner, too, and a confidant—as well as a critic and an instructor. When I pressed her to explain these last losses further, she said sadly and softly, "My self-esteem, as a woman and as a person, was all tied up with his reactions to me. I didn't just lose a husband. I lost my way of evaluating myself. He was my mirror. Now I don't know how I look any more."

It is not underestimating the seriousness of her other losses to say that this was the biggest one. But neither is it underestimating the gravity of the loss of her mirror, as she called it, to say that it represented an opportunity for development. It was a long time before we called it that, however, for the natural process of grieving is sometimes a very slow one. But within a few weeks she was beginning to talk about a sense that she occasionally had that she had come to a time in her life where she did not need to rely so much on others for a sense of how she was doing. This view of things grew on her, and she discussed it more frequently, until one day she came in and announced that she had decided that the divorce was no random accident in her life. "Any earlier and I'd have not been ready; any later and I'd have been so hopelessly invested in our system that I'd have died when it was broken. Yes, it came just at the right moment."

Connie's life transition was a turning point in her life, leaving her a stronger and more vital person than she had been before. It had begun with an ending, and the ending had begun with a disengagement. Connie had been deprived of the familiar ways of knowing herself by the separation from her husband, and this provided her with an opportunity that would have been hard to find within their relationship. (This is not to say that a divorce was necessary—only that some significant disengagement was an important element in making her change.)

Divorces, deaths, job changes, moves, illnesses, and many lesser events disengage us from the contexts in which we have known ourselves. They break up the old cue-system which served to reinforce our roles and to pattern our behavior. It isn't just that the disappearance of the old system forces us to devise a new one, the way that a breakdown in the economic order might lead to barter. It is rather that as long as a system is working, it is very hard for any member of it to imagine an alternative way of life and an alternative identity. But with disengagement, an inexorable process of change begins. Clarified, channeled, and supported, that change can lead toward development and renewal.

Disidentification

In breaking the old connections to the world, the person loses ways of self-definition. Connie's way of putting it had been that she had "lost her mirror." Others feel it as a loss of a role that prescribed their behavior and made them readily identifiable, while still others feel the lack of a familiar and identifying label. One way or another, most people in transition have the experience of not being quite sure who they are any more. This experience corresponds to an important element in most passage ceremonies: the removal of the signs of the old identity and the temporary assumption of a sort of non-identity, represented by shaved heads, painted faces, masks, strange clothing or no clothing at all, or the abandonment of one's old name.

In most cases this disidentification process is really the inner side of the disengagement process. It is often particularly distressing in vocational transitions, or in cases where the old roles and titles were an important part of the person's identity. The impact of such losses can be much greater than one imagines in advance.

I had thought about this loss a good deal when I was leaving my teaching career, for example, and I was convinced that I had thought it through and had come to terms with "not being a teacher any more." Then one day my youngest daughter asked casually, "What are you, Daddy?" I began one of those long and careful replies that rapidly exhaust the child's interest in the subject. I told her how I used to be a teacher (the past comes in handy when the present isn't very clear) and how I was now partly a lecturer and partly a writer, and I did counseling and consulting, and . . . . Then, seeing that I was losing her, I said, "Why do you ask?" "Oh, we're talking at school about what our daddies do, and I wondered what I should say."

This troubled me for weeks. I had thought that I was comfortable with my temporary state of disidentification, but I found that I was vulnerable through the kids—who didn't really care *what* I did, so long as it had a name. As time went on, I grew more comfortable with what might be called a "participial" identity, that is identifying with *-ing* words (gardening, writing, running, lecturing) rather than nouns. But I have to admit that it always bothered me that the kids preferred nouns. They corresponded to that part of me that still longed for the lost security of a recognizable label. Teacher, college professor, the Aurelia Henry Reinhardt Professor of American Literature at Mills College. Ah, those were the old days! But now, gardening . . . running . . . ? ("Whatever happened to Bridges, anyhow?")

It often gave me pleasure during that period to imagine that I was in the middle of a secret passage ritual. In a world of social identities, I was an interloper. I lived in the cracks and moved in the shadows. My own passage markings were hidden and secret, but I was being initiated into the next phase of my life—into middle age, for lack of a better term. I had cast the shell of my old identity like a lobster, and I was staying close to the rocks because

I was still soft and vulnerable. I'd have a new and better fitting identity in time, but for now I'd have to go a little slowly.

I found it useful then to reflect more seriously on why being disidentified was an important part of the termination process. Clearly, the old identity stands in the way of transition—and of transformation and self-renewal. I could appreciate the wry wisdom in the sign that Erik Erikson reports having seen over a bar in a western town: "I ain't what I ought to be," it read, "and I ain't what I'm going to be. But I ain't what I was!"

At other times, though, disidentification is no laughing matter. No longer being *Bob's wife* or *a salesman,* no longer being the *old me* or *a young person* is a source of panic. That is when it is important to remember the significance of disidentification and the need to loosen the bonds of who we think we are so that we can go through a transition toward a new identity.

Disenchantment

Separated from the old identity and the old situation or some important aspect of it, a person floats free in a kind of limbo between two worlds. But there is still the reality in that person's head—a picture of the "way things are," which ties the person to the old world with subtle strands of assumption and expectation. The sun will rise tomorrow, my mother loves me, the tribe will endure, the gods are just: These things are *so,* and if they are not my world is no longer real. The discovery that in some sense one's world is indeed no longer real is what is meant by disenchantment.

In traditional rites of passage disenchantment was a

carefully arranged experience.[3] In the ceremony for entry into the healing cult of the Ndembu of Africa, initiates are brought before a strange shape in the jungle, which they are told is Kavula, or the cult's spirit. Then unexpectedly they are told to beat on the spirit-shape with sticks and kill it. At the end they are shown that the thing being beaten is nothing but a cloth-covered frame under which adepts have been hiding. A similar process takes place in other passage ceremonies: when Hopi youths see the awe-inspiring kachinas (who are neighbors and relatives) unmask for the first time or when terrified initiates in aboriginal Australia are shown that the fearful sound of the great spirit Dhuramoolan is nothing more than a bullroarer, or flat piece of wood on a thong.

This may remind you of the disenchantments of your own childhood: that there is no Santa Claus; that parents sometimes lie and are afraid and make stupid mistakes and like silly things; that best friends let you down. But these disenchantments did not end with childhood—nor are they over yet. The lifetime contains a long chain of disenchantments, many small and a few large: lovers who proved unfaithful, leaders who were corrupt, idols who turned out to be petty and dull, organizations that betrayed your trust. Worst of all, there are the times when you yourself turned out to be what you said and even believed that you were not. Disenchantment, you can quickly discover, is a recurrent experience throughout the lifetime of anyone who has the courage and trust to believe in the first place.

Many significant transitions not only involve disenchantment, they begin with it. But like the other aspects of the termination process, it may be only slowly that the person can begin to see the disenchantment experience as meaningful. When you discover the fatal love letter or get the news that you've been fired, it's pointless to talk about old realities and new ones. But later it is important to reflect on these things, for with realities as with identities and connections, the old must be cleared away before the new can grow. The mind is a vessel that must be emptied if new wine is to be put in.

This process is hard to take in more than just a natural, personal sense, for it goes against the grain of our culture, which tends to view growth as an additive process. We did not have to unlearn the first grade to go on to the second, for example, or forget Sunday school to join the church. We do not expect to have to give up old beliefs (in spite of St. Paul's injunction to "put away childish things") in order to mature. In fact, the whole termination process violates our too-seldom examined idea that development means gain and has nothing to do with loss.

The Western mind has worked this way for a long time. Odysseus, you will remember, found it terribly difficult to let go of his assumptions about reality. The world was a battlefield and requires armor and struggle. He had been a winner by those rules, and it made no sense to him suddenly to find them not working at Ismaros or in the narrows between Scylla and Charybdis. He found that the first task of transition was unlearning, not learning anew.

The lesson of disenchantment begins with the discovery that in order to change—really to change, and not just to switch positions—you must realize that some significant part of your old reality was in your head, not out there. The flawless parent, the noble leader, the perfect wife, the utterly trustworthy friend are an *inner* cast of characters looking for actors to play the parts. One person is after someone older and wiser, and another is after an admiring follower. And when they find each other they fit like the interlocking pieces of a puzzle.

Or almost. Actually, the misfit is greater than either

person knows or even wants to know. The thing that keeps this misperception in place is an "enchantment," a spell cast by the past on the present. Most of these enchantments work fairly well, but at life's turning points they break down. Almost inevitably we feel cheated at such times, as though someone were trying to trick us. But usually the earlier enchanted view was as "real" as we could manage at the time. It corresponded to a self-image and a situation, and it could not change without affecting self and others.

The point is that disenchantment, whether it is a minor disappointment or a major shock, is the signal that things are moving into transition. At such times we need to consider whether the old view or belief may not have been an enchantment cast on us in the past to keep us from seeing deeper into ourselves and others than we were then ready to. For the whole idea of disenchantment is that reality has many layers, each appropriate to a phase of intellectual and spiritual development. The disenchantment experience is the signal that the time has come to look below the surface of what has been thought to be *so*.

Lacking this perspective on such experiences, however, we often miss the point and simply become "disillusioned." The disenchanted person recognizes the old view as sufficient in its time, but insufficient now: "I needed to believe that husbands [or friends or mentors] were always trustworthy; it protected me against some of the contingencies of life." On the other hand, the disillusioned person simply rejects the embodiment of the earlier view: She gets a new husband or he gets a new boss, but both leave unchanged the old enchanted view of relationships. The disenchanted person moves on, but the disillusioned person stops and goes through the play again with new actors. Such a person is on a perpetual quest for a *real* friend, a *true* mate, and a *trustworthy* leader. The quest only goes around in circles, and real movement and real development are arrested.

Disorientation

The "reality" that is left behind in any ending is not just a picture on the wall. It is a sense of which way is up and which way is down; it is a sense of which way is forward and which way is backward. It is, in short, a way of orienting oneself and of moving forward into the future. In the old passage rituals, the one in transition often would be taken out into unfamiliar territory beyond the bounds of his or her experience and left there for a time. All the customary signs of location would be gone, and the only remaining source of orientation would be the heavens. In such a setting and the state of mind it was meant to create, you would be (in the words of Robert Frost) "lost enough to find yourself."

As with other aspects of the ending process, most of us already know the disorientation experience. We recognize the lost, confused, don't-know-where-I-am feeling that deepens as we become disengaged, disidentified, and disenchanted. The old sense of life as "going somewhere" breaks down, and we feel like shipwrecked sailors on some existential atoll.

One of the first and most serious casualties of disorientation is our sense of and plans for the future. The guy who is fired (disengagement) or bypassed for promotion one last time (disenchantment) is likely to find himself losing interest in old goals and plans. This loss of motive power and direction is frightening to many individuals and those around them, and it may in fact be dangerous in a practical sense if it threatens the essential arrangements of a person's life.

It would be a mistake in such situations to view disorientation as positively as one can in retrospect. Traditional people in passage did not enjoy or embrace the experience of disorientation. They suffered through it because *that was the way,* which is to say because they had faith in the death and rebirth process. Having that faith they did not need to try to make distress comfortable. However, many modern people lacking that faith are caught between positive thinking and despair, keeping themselves going by lighting matches and whistling in the dark.

There is a danger that what I am saying about disorientation and the ending process in general will become merely a rationalization or an anesthetic for personal distress. ("Hey, isn't that wonderful! I just bumped into a tree. I must be *disoriented!*") To do that is to deny the real experience and to vitiate the transition process. Disorientation is meaningful, but it isn't enjoyable. It is a time of confusion and emptiness when ordinary things have an unreal quality about them. Things that used to be important don't seem to matter much now. We feel stuck, dead, lost in some great, dark non-world. No wonder that many myths depict this state as one in which the hero is swallowed and trapped in the entrails of a great serpent or fish. No wonder that a hero's path at that point was the convoluted way through a labyrinth.

Disorientation affects not only our sense of space but our sense of time as well. I talked with a man recently who had just stopped smoking. "Where did all the extra time come from?" he asked half seriously. "I must have used up hours and hours smoking." And that is so, to some extent. But the changed time sense also comes from the ending of a familiar way of structuring time. A couple of times an hour this man was used to taking out matches and cigarettes and going through a familiar set of actions. Although time-lapses between cigarettes might have varied, he could have marked the passage of time by the butts in the ashtray. When he stopped smoking, time stretched before him like the open sea.

That often happens in transition, and some of our resistance to going into transition comes from our fear of this emptiness. The problem is not that we don't want to give up a job or a relationship, or that we can't let go of our identity or our reality; the problem is that before we can find a new something, we must deal with a time of nothing. And that prospect awakens old fears and all the old fantasies about death and abandonment.

The Oedipus complex— another view

The ancient story of Oedipus is full of wisdom concerning the way in which a phase of life comes to an end. We are most familiar with interpretations of the myth as an account of the effects of romantic rivalry in childhood— Freud having said that all men wish to destroy their fathers and marry their mothers. But Sophocles' *Oedipus Rex* seems to me to disclose much about life in general if it is viewed as a myth about the transition process. Because we need to set aside our preconceptions about this play if we are to see it afresh, I suggest that we view it not as a famous tragedy or as the basis for psychoanalytic theory, but as it would be if it were your own dream. In viewing it that way, it will also be possible to relate it more directly to the deeper levels of your own experience.

Imagine that you wake suddenly in the middle of the night and lie there, frightened and confused by a strange dream. In it, you are standing in a great square, surrounded by the facades of temples and palaces. Before you is a large crowd of townspeople, some kneeling or standing, and some lying down with illness and fatigue. All of them are looking at you with a mixture of desperate hope and fear in their eyes. They are silent except for an occasional child's whimper or a moan from one of the sick. Wordlessly these people are beseeching you to save them from something.

Then a spokesman steps forth from the group and addresses you directly. Calling you *ruler,* he says that the city is under a curse. The crops are withering in the fields, and the herds are weak and dying. Women are bearing stillborn children, and sickness is everywhere.

Before you have time to reply, he reminds you how you came to be the ruler of this land. The city was at that time, too, in the grip of a curse, as the terrible sphinx crouched outside the city gate and refused to give back life to the city until someone answered the sphinx's riddle about the animal that walks on four feet in the morning, two at noon, and three in the evening. You were young then, just beginning to make your own way in the world, and you stepped forth and risked an answer: *the human being,* you said. You solved the riddle, the spell was broken, and in gratitude the city made you its ruler.

So now the spokesman says, "Do it for us again." [In the actual play, he puts it even more cunningly: "Never be it our memory of thy reign that we were first restored and afterward cast down by you."] They are asking you to keep on being the one you have always been—to live up to your public image. They ask you not to change now.

And that is where the dream ends, but long after you have risen the dream stays with you, nagging at you and drawing your attention away from the practical business of waking life. What a compelling argument: Do it again . . . don't change now . . . live up to your image . . . keep on being the old *you.* The dream and its argument stir something deep in you. It blends with your daily activity in a strange way that becomes something suggestive. Holding the dream-shape in your mind, you think about what is going on with you just now. Dream and life correspond somehow, like a sketch and a face. And then you realize . . .

From home, from work, even from your own mind comes the appeal to keep on being the one you've been. Don't change. Do the old, familiar thing again. Just at this point in life when you feel drawn toward new beginnings, there are these powerful inner and outer forces blocking the way. The dream is your life.

The Oedipal situation, viewed in this context, is not the triangular pattern of mother, father, and child, but rather the situation of the adult who is torn between the developmental thrust that brings about life transitions and the impulse toward repetition that aborts them. Viewed symbolically, the withering crops and the stillborn creatures are signs of the dying of an old life phase and the feelings of deadness that so often signal the beginning of the termination process.

The story of Oedipus is thus a symbolic representation of what goes on in our lives when we seek to hold on to an old and outlived way of being in the world. It is that old way that is the source of the curse, as Oedipus finds when he sends for counsel from the oracle at Delphi. The oracle says that a "defiling thing" is the cause, and that thing is the presence in the city of the murderer of the former king. Now, that murderer is Oedipus himself, for on his way to the city twenty years before, he had encountered a man at a narrow place in the road and argued with him over the right of way. The older man tried to run him down, and the young Oedipus fought back and killed him—not knowing that the man was King Laius.

But the killing itself wasn't the source of the trouble, for the gods brought Oedipus to the city, placed the right answer in his mouth, made him a hero, and let Thebes prosper for twenty years under his scepter. Viewed symbolically, that killing was the natural and necessary act of its time. Like many actual parents, this mythic father blocked his son's way and denied his right to emerge into his own. Becoming independent and finding his own place in the world entailed a symbolic slaying of the parent and the dependency that had once been necessary.

But Oedipus had long since finished with that developmental business. That phase of life (the *heroic* phase, in mythic terms) is done and something else is ready to take its place. This natural and inexorable succession of life phases was, as we noted in Chapter 2, the very point of the sphinx's riddle. Like many of us, Oedipus knew the "answer" but failed to apply it in the crucial and complex life situation.

For Oedipus is exactly at the second great transition point in life, the time when he must leave the involvement and identification with the social roles and self-images that have been successful. Now, however, there is no outer enemy. There is only the puzzle-solving, dragon-slaying man who sees the world in terms of outer enemies—a man trying to perpetuate an outlived way of being and acting.

So what does he do? He sends to Delphi for the answer. (The old puzzle-solver will set things right.) And the answer is that the murderer of Laius is defiling the city. Oedipus announces that he will find the man and he will banish him. (The hero rides again!) He brings to bear on this time of life transition the very approach to things that life is calling upon him to give up. And in the process, the hero slays "the hero" in himself.

The story of Oedipus illuminates the process of life transition. It shows that after a certain point the very ways of being that brought forth a life phase begin to destroy it. This happens more than once in the play. Oedipus had been sent away shortly after birth because of a prophecy that he would one day kill his father. And he later left his foster parents' house when he heard about that prophecy. At each step, the attempt to perpetuate something is the act that initiates its downfall. Our endings, we must discover, are often brought about by the very acts and words that we believed would keep things going.

There is, the myth suggests, a morality that is deeper than any code of social ethics, and it comes from a natural order that moves to the rhythm of life itself. The goal of one phase of life becomes the burden of the next. That is why rites of passage begin with a symbolic death. Without that death, the life becomes "polluted," as the oracle said the city of Thebes had become.

Having so strenuously resisted the summons to change, Oedipus suffered terribly in the process of transformation. But we often forget that there is a sequel to *Oedipus Rex* and that Sophocles meant us to see that after the death came a rebirth and a new way of being in the world. By the time we meet Oedipus again in *Oedipus at Colonus,* he has passed through the suffering of loss. Leaning on the cane that the sphinx's riddle had referred to, he is not just old but is spiritually enlightened and a blessing to whatever town harbors him.

Oedipus's story makes us realize that we are likely to resist and misunderstand significant transitional changes—at a time when it is terribly important to seek another perspective. Oedipus sent to Delphi for counsel, but he misread the oracle's reply. He called in the great seer Tiresias but he refused to hear what the sage told him. He tried to fit the new information into his old reality, but in the end the disenchantment took place and he understood what had happened.

The experience of the ending

Endings begin with something going wrong. At Ismaros, Odysseus failed where he had always succeeded before. At Thebes, Oedipus experienced a subtler and more pervasive loss—a deadening, a withering, a loss of vitality. For one person an ending may be an event, while for another it may be a state of mind.

Nor do the elements in an ending come in any particular order. In a divorce, for example, one partner may experience disidentification and disorientation and then decide to act—which leads to disengagement. For the other partner, unaware of the impending change, the ending begins with disengagement and the challenge of disenchantment. There is no natural or normal order.

Nor is there any normal order of reactions to an ending. Some people react to endings the same way that Elisabeth Kubler-Ross found terminally ill patients reacting to their impending deaths: in a five stage sequence that moves from denial to anger to bargaining to depression to acceptance.[4] One can see that general course of response in the case of Oedipus. But others seem to reverse this course, starting with acceptance and discovering only much later that they are losing anything in the transition.

The point is that it is important to let ourselves or others in transition react to endings. You are not the first person who ever lost a job (or moved or had heart surgery), but telling you that is no help. If you keep acting that way, I can only conclude that you just can't let go of something in this process. You may well need help, perhaps professional help, but you don't need me to tell you to stop crying over spilt milk and put on a happy face.

Endings are, let's remember, experiences of dying. They are ordeals, and sometimes they challenge so basically our sense of who we are that we believe they will be the end of *us*. This is where an understanding of endings and some familiarity with the old passage rituals can be helpful. For as Mircea Eliade, one of the greatest students of these rituals, has written, "In no rite or myth do we find the initiatory death as something *final*, but always as the condition *sine qua non* of a transition to another mode of being, a trial indispensable to regeneration; that is, to the beginning of a new life."[5]

5

THE NEUTRAL ZONE

I do my utmost to attain emptiness; I hold firmly to stillness. (XVI)

Do that which consists in taking no action; pursue that which is not meddlesome; savour that which has no flavour. (LXIII)

LAO TZU
Tao Te Ching[1]

In other times and places the person in transition left the village and went out into an unfamiliar stretch of forest or desert. There the person would remain for a time, removed from the old connections, bereft of the old identities, and stripped of the old reality. This was a time "between dreams" in which the old chaos from the beginnings welled up and obliterated all forms. It was a place without a name—an empty space in the world and the lifetime within which a new sense of self could gestate.

One of the difficulties of being in transition in the modern world is that we have lost our appreciation for this gap in the continuity of existence. For us, emptiness represents only the absence of something. So when the *something* is as important as relatedness and purpose and reality, we try to find ways of replacing these missing elements as quickly as possible. The neutral zone is not an important part of the transition process—it is only a temporary state of loss to be endured.

In this view, transition is a kind of street-crossing procedure. One would be a fool to stay out there in the middle of the street any longer than was necessary, so once you step off the curb, move on to the other side as fast as you can. And whatever you do, don't sit down on the center line to think things over!

No wonder we have so much difficulty with our transitions. This view makes no sense out of the pain of ending, for all that we can imagine is that our distress is a sign that we should not have crossed the street in the first place. It also makes no sense out of the feeling of lostness that we are likely to experience or the feeling that the emptiness seems to stretch on forever. ("Wait a minute," we want to object. "There *is* another side to this street, isn't there?") And as for transition as a source of self-renewal, well, after you've struggled and floundered across a scary place like that, you *need* some self-renewal.

Yet even as we distort and misunderstand the neutral zone experience, we live it out unwittingly. Without quite knowing why, people in the middle of transition tend to find ways of being alone and away from all the familiar distractions. Perhaps it is a long weekend in a borrowed cabin on a lake, or perhaps it is a few days alone in a city hotel. One member of that first transition class had just returned from four days ("the strangest four days in my life," she called them) backpacking alone in the mountains. "Where can we reach you?" her husband asked with concern. The woman, who had never before gone anywhere by herself, replied simply, "You can't. But I'll be back."

Whenever they ask, we tell the people being left behind that we just want to get away by ourselves for a little while—which is probably as much as we ourselves know at the time. They may have their own anxious fantasies of what we are really doing—meeting a secret lover, going off to end it all, or abandoning them to begin life under a new identity elsewhere. (And, in fact, we ourselves may be playing with one or more of these possibilities in our own fantasies.)

If we do tell them where we are going, they ask in genuine puzzlement, "What are you going to *do* there all alone?" We hardly know what to answer, though, for we are heading down a dark pathway in our lives at that point. "I want time to think things over, I guess," we say a little lamely. But then it turns out that once we are out there we don't really *think* in any way that produces definite results. Instead, we walk the beaches or the back streets. We sit in the park or the movies. We watch the people and the clouds. "I didn't do much of anything," we report on our return. And we feel a little defensive, as though we had failed to deliver what we had promised.

We need not feel defensive about this apparently unproductive time-out at turning points in our lives, for the neutral zone is meant to be a moratorium from the conventional activity of our everyday existence. It is that activity that keeps us "us" by presenting us with a set of signals that are very difficult to respond to in any but the old way. In the apparently aimless activity of our time alone, we are doing important inner business. Walking, watching, making coffee, counting the birds on the phone wire, studying the cracks in the plaster ceiling over the bed, dreaming, waiting for God knows what to happen, we carry on the basic industry of the neutral zone, which is attentive inactivity and ritualized routine.

In the old passage rituals, people were brought up and educated to know what to do in these natural but mysterious gaps in the lifetime. They learned to solicit the aid of dream figures—so-called spirit-guides of one sort or another. They were instructed in symbolic modes of perception, wherein the whole natural order became a symbolic communication written for their enlightenment and guidance. They learned to cultivate mental states in which heightened kinds of awareness were possible— sometimes by means of meditation and chanting, sometimes with fasting and dehydration in the sweat-lodge, and sometimes with the aid of psychotropic substances.

A modern account of such instruction is given in Carlos Castaneda's books about Don Juan and the Yaqui teachings. Whether these are taken as fact or as fiction, they represent an unusually rich account of a modern westerner's encounter with the neutral zone experience in its starkest and most powerful form. One finds descriptions of the teaching and the resulting experiences almost anywhere one opens the four books. I open the first at random and find:

> *Don Juan waited awhile and then, going through the same motions, handed me the lizards again. He told me to hold their heads up and rub them softly against my temples, as I asked them anything I wanted to know. I did not understand at first what he wanted me to do. . . . He gave me a whole series of examples: I could find out about persons I did not see ordinarily, or about objects that were lost, or about places I had not seen. Then I realized he was talking about* divination. *I got very excited. My heart began to pound. I felt that I was losing my breath.*[2]

Such ways of knowing are so alien to most of us that they seem bizarre and even frightening. But in fact many ordinary members of our own culture have similar experiences of extraordinary kinds of awareness in their own neutral zones. Lacking guidance and validation at such times, many people discount these experiences and some are deeply troubled by them.

One of the members of the first transition class was a former electrical engineer named Pat, a man in his forties, who said little about himself except that he had "dropped out of the rat race," as he put it. Bit by bit, we discovered that he had been laid off by a space-industry firm and had separated from his wife a few months later, after bitter disagreements about his lack of initiative in finding another job. "I didn't want to lose that job," he said one night, "but once it was gone, I realized that I didn't want another like it. I didn't know what I did want, and my wife found my indecisiveness too frustrating—so she left."

All of this was said with so little feeling that one would have thought he was talking about someone else's life. But when he shifted to the subject of the present and his strange experiences, he came quickly to life again. It seemed that his whole reality had changed. He had never dreamed much before, but now he was dreaming every night. He had had several experiences of "seeing," as he called it. "Seeing" meant really understanding what his life was all about and why he had lost his job and his marriage. "I feel as though I've broken through a wall and can see the world for the first time," he said with real feeling.

Some members of the class dismissed Pat as someone who'd gone off the deep end, but others said that they knew what he was talking about. His honesty made it easier for others to talk, and we shortly discovered that the encounter with another level of reality was not uncommon in our group. Some chalked it up to a great activation of their imaginations, others to some new access to areas of their consciousness that they hadn't been aware of before, and a few argued for actual contact with spiritual presences. "You can say anything you want to about it," one woman said defiantly, "but I've found out that I have a guide that I can talk to when I get into the right frame of mind."

What we were discovering that night, and what too few people in transition have the opportunity to hear, is

116

that for many people the breakdown of the old "enchant-ment" and the old self-image uncovers a hitherto unsus-pected kind of awareness. Not everyone in transition has this experience, but it is common enough to suggest that the old consciousness-altering techniques used in rites of passage did not *create* a different reality, but only en-hanced the natural tendency to see and understand the world differently in the gap between one life phase and the next.

This is an important discovery, for too many people either deny this aspect of the neutral zone experience or else become overwhelmed by it. To deny it is to lose the opportunity it provides for an expanded sense of reality and a deepened sense of purpose. And to be overwhelmed by it is just as unfortunate, for one then has no way to integrate the experience with the rest of one's life. In either case, the transition process fails to provide the per-son with the enrichment that is one of its natural but almost forgotten gifts.

In taking the initiate out into the wilderness and ener-vating him or her with fasting and fatigue, in suppressing the initiate's old consciousness with chanting and rhyth-mical movements, in enlivening the imagination with mythic tales and symbolical procedures of various sorts—in all these ways, traditional societies opened the person to the transformative experience of the neutral zone. Fur-thermore, they made that experience intelligible and ca-pable of assimilation. With us, however, it's a hit-or-miss affair at best. We aren't sure what is happening to us or when it will be over. We don't know whether we are going crazy or becoming enlightened, and neither prospect is one that we can readily discuss with anyone else.

For many people the experience of the neutral zone is essentially one of emptiness in which the old reality looks transparent and nothing feels solid any more. Leo Tolstoy left us with a powerful description of his own encounter with that nothingness: "I felt," he wrote, "that something had broken within me on which my life had always rested, that I had nothing left to hold on to, and that morally my life had stopped." He became obsessed with the thought of death and went so far as to give up hunting for fear that he would turn the gun on himself one day. Outwardly his life showed little sign of change:

> And yet I could give no reasonable meaning to any actions of my life. And I was surprised that I had not understood this from the very beginning. My state of mind was as if some wicked and stupid jest was being played upon me by someone. . . . [I asked myself] what will be the outcome of what I do today? Of what I shall do tomorrow? What will be the outcome of all my life? Why should I live? Why should I do anything?[3]

There, right under the surface of his everyday life, Tolstoy had discovered the great emptiness of the neutral zone.

I sometimes wonder what would have happened if Tolstoy had brought his anguish to a conventional therapist—and I imagine exchanges like the following:

"When did you first notice this 'wicked and stupid jest,' as you call it?"

"I've felt it for weeks."

"Have you always suspected that people were making fun of you this way?"

Or: "How are things between you and Mrs. Tolstoy these days?"

Or: "Tell me something about your childhood."

Or, just as bad as these but more current: "Well, now, Leo—you don't mind if I call you Leo, do you?—we call these difficult times, 'mid-life crises.' "

Perhaps Tolstoy was just as well off having to do

without the assistance of the psychoanalyst. Be that as it may, he clearly could have used help—someone who could appreciate his suffering and his confusion, some way of making sense out of it, some route to follow through it. He could have endured his situation a little better, perhaps, if he had realized that the emptiness that he experienced was the natural result of the ending process and that the ground was now ready for the emergence of new life. He could have felt a little less alone if he had realized how common his experience was. And he could have faced the future more confidently if he had had some tools with which to clear a pathway for himself through the wilderness.

These "tools" were once provided by the tribal elders in the form of instruction and ritual, but we must fashion our own tools today. It is tempting to think that we can recover and reanimate lost rituals, but that seldom works very well. Rather, we need to understand what neutral-zone activities the old rituals facilitated and then discover our own ways of doing those things.

The first of the neutral-zone activities or functions is surrender—the person must give in to the emptiness and stop struggling to escape it. This is not easy, although it is made easier by an understanding of why the emptiness is essential. There are three main reasons for the emptiness between the old life and the new. First, the process of transformation is essentially a death and rebirth process rather than one of mechanical modification. While our own culture knows all about mechanics, it has a great deal to learn from the past about death and rebirth. As Mircea Eliade has written, "for the archaic and traditional cultures, the symbolic return to chaos is indispensable to any new Creation."[4] Chaos is not a mess, but rather it is the primal state of pure energy to which the person returns for every true new beginning. It is only from the perspective of the old form that chaos looks fearful—from

119

any other perspective, it looks like life itself, as yet un-shaped by purpose and identification.

The second reason for the gap between the old life and the new is that the process of disintegration and reintegration is the source of renewal. As van Gennep noted in his seminal *Rites of Passage*:

> *Although a body can move through space in a circle at a constant speed, the same is not true of biological or social activities. Their energy becomes exhausted, and they have to be regenerated at more or less close intervals. The rites of passage ultimately correspond to this fundamental necessity.*[5]

In our age of stress, alienation, and burnout, this is surely a piece of wisdom that we need to recover. In keeping with our mechanistic bias, we have tried to make do with re-charging and repair, imagining that renewal comes through fixing something defective or supplying something that is missing. In fact it is only by returning for a time to the formlessness of the primal energy that renewal can take place. The neutral zone is the only source of the self-renewal that we all seek.

The last reason for the emptiness between the stages of the life journey is the perspective it provides on the stages themselves. Viewed from that emptiness, the realities of the everyday world look transparent and insub-stantial, and we can see what is meant by the statement that everything is "illusion." Few of us can live in the harsh light of this knowledge for long, but even when we return to the engagements and identifications of ordinary "reality," we carry with us an appreciation of the un-knowable ground beyond every image. The neutral zone provides access to an angle of vision on life that one can get nowhere else. And it is a succession of such views over a lifetime that produces wisdom.

You may feel this is heavy stuff—and it is. You only wanted a little help getting out of this strange crack between life's floorboards that you unexpectedly fell into. Well, first you've got to understand what you're doing there, and then you've got to see why it's important to stay there for a while—and *then* we can talk about what to do.

For "what to do" consists not of ways out but of ways in—that is, it involves ways of amplifying and making more real the essential neutral zone experience. The way out *is* the way in, as it happens. When the wheels spin in loose gravel, you need more weight. Tempting though it may be to do something else and wait for the experience to pass, it turns out that it is one of those things that is going to wait around until it gets your attention. So here are some practical suggestions of how to find the meaning in the neutral-zone experience—and thus how to shorten it.

1. *Find a regular time and place to be alone.* People in transition are often still involved in activities and relationships that continue to bombard them with cues that are irrelevant to their emerging needs. Because a person is likely to feel lonely in such a situation, the temptation is to seek more and better contact with others; but the real need is for a genuine sort of aloneness in which inner signals can make themselves heard. Doing housework after the kids leave for school or doing paperwork with the office door shut are not being alone in the sense I am talking about.

The old passage rituals provided the person with this experience of aloneness all in one piece, but it is likely that you will have to cut it to fit the actuality of your own life situation. One person manages it by getting up every morning forty-five minutes ahead of the rest of the family and sitting quietly in the living room with a cup of coffee.

Another jogs regularly after work for half an hour. Another has cassettes of ocean sounds and temple bells that he plays on his car stereo whenever he drives alone for any distance. Still another has cleaned out a little storage room off the upstairs hall and sits quietly alone in there for an hour after supper with a Do Not Disturb sign on the door.

2. *Begin a log of neutral-zone experiences.* Lost in the welter of moment-to-moment incident, the important experiences of the neutral zone are often difficult to see. But looking back, at the end of a day or a week, they may stand out, like a path through the grass that was all but invisible as you walked it. The approach you take to logging these experiences is important, however, because it can easily degenerate into a trivial kind of diary-keeping. What you want to capture is a day or a week of your experience: What was *really* going on? What was your mood? What were you thinking about, perhaps without realizing it, at the time? What puzzling or unusual things happened? What decisions do you wish you could have made? What dreams do you remember having?

"But you don't see," says the man who comes up after the lecture for advice. "I'm nowhere and I want to get somewhere. This neutral zone—there's nothing here to record." Yes, it is a paradox, I agree: To talk about emptiness and then to suggest that there is something there worth noting. The point is that we need to resist the tendency to imagine that what is needed is external to our situation. As Ralph Waldo Emerson put it, "Every man's condition is a solution in hieroglyphic to those inquiries he would put. He acts it as life, before he apprehends it as truth."[6]

3. *Take this pause in the action of your life to write an autobiography.* You, an autobiographer? Why you, why now? Because sometimes it is only in seeing where you have been that you can tell where you are headed. Be-

cause reminiscence is a natural impulse whenever something has just ended, as though you cannot really terminate anything without reviewing it and putting it into order. Because recollection is likely to turn up some useful information about other transitions in your past. And because your past is out of date and needs revision.

What you call your *past* is a tiny portion of your actual living, a selection of situation and event that is supposed to account for the *present*. One of George Orwell's slogans in *1984* was, "Who controls the present controls the past; who controls the past controls the future."[7] Beneath his cynicism (history was always being self-consciously "revised" there, you remember), Orwell notes that it is the present situation that makes a given past make sense—and that a given past suggests a particular future. Even when we set out to change the present, it is the past that defines the possibilities and the limits of the change.

Thus it is important in times of transition to reflect on the past for a number of reasons—not least of which is that from the perspective of a new present, the past is likely to look different. For the past isn't like a landscape or a vase of flowers that is just *there*. It is more like the raw material awaiting a builder.

Let's say you were born in Pittsburgh and you had two sisters, and your grandmother died in 1953—or was it 1954? Well, it was about the time that your father took the long business trip (he brought back sweaters to all of you, remember?), and your mother was acting depressed. When you ask your older sister about this, she remembers that your parents had a big fight just before your father left, and she wonders if the trip wasn't really a separation. (How come that never occurred to you?)

Well, anyway, that makes it 1953, and . . . wait. Maybe they did separate, because you were sent off unexpectedly to stay with your uncle that summer—and you almost stayed when they offered you the job at the coffee shop. Boy, that was a real crossroads in your life, although you didn't know it then. (What do you suppose would have happened if you *had* stayed and hadn't started college the next year?)

You can't follow the thread of your life very far before you find "the past" changing. Things that you haven't remembered in years reappear, and things that you've always thought were *so,* turn out to be not so at all. If the past isn't the way you thought it was, then the present isn't either. Letting go of that present may make it easier to conceive of a new future. Things look different from the neutral zone, for one of the things you let go of in the ending process is the need to see the past in a particular way.

4. *Take this opportunity to discover what you really want.* What *do* you want, anyway? When the circumstances of our lives box us in, we usually assume that we know what we want but simply cannot get it. "If only I could. . . ." The refrain is familiar. In times of transition however, a distressing change often takes place: The limiting circumstances are part of what ends, and we are no longer held back from doing what we want to do. But now the refrain changes: "If only I knew what I really wanted . . . ."

Wanting turns out to be a far less clear matter than we usually imagine, for it is overlayed with a lifetime of guilt and ambivalence. As children we may have been told that we were selfish or that we were never satisfied with what we got. Or perhaps we were told that we only *thought* we knew what we wanted. ("You don't really want that . . . When you're older, you'll realize . . . You *really* want to please Mommy, don't you?") Or else the simple pain of disappointment grew too great as our wants were disregarded time after time, and we learned to protect ourselves by blocking off an awareness of our wantings.

124

So here we are now, in a position to get a little of what we want after all these years, and we find ourselves unsure and confused. How can we get past this difficulty and use our real wantings to orient us toward the future? By understanding how we characteristically suppress our wantings and how to stop doing that. To do these things, try this:

Imagine that you are going to get yourself something to eat or drink right now. (Assume for the moment that you can actually have anything you want—all the ordinary problems of cost and supply are taken care of.) Now, stop reading for just a moment and think: "What do I really want to eat or drink right now?" (Take one or two minutes to think about that before you read any further.)

What did you do with that question? Forget the answer that you did or did not come up with, and think instead about the answer-getting process. How did you go about it:

1. Did you consult your mouth or your stomach or your mind?
2. Did you try to *figure out* the answer, as though it were a question on a history test?
3. Did you imagine a menu and run over the possibilities—hamburger, no . . . french fries, too greasy . . . ice cream, too fattening . . . .
4. Did you try to remember something good you had eaten recently?
5. Did you try to recall your "favorite food"?
6. Did you come up with an answer and then shelve it because it was silly or strange?

Some people seem to know instinctively what they want, and they usually get their signals from their mouths or their stomachs. However, most people use some strategy to "come up with an answer." If you are one of those people, the chances are good that you do the same thing when it comes to far more important wantings and that here and now, in the neutral zone, you are not letting yourself know what you really want out of your life.[8]

5. *Think of what would be unlived in your life if it ended today.* Suppose that a tree fell on you right now or that you had sudden heart failure. There. It's all over. Your life is complete. Whatever you've done is the *you* that goes down in the record books, and everything you might have done vanishes with the mind that considered it. Imagine that you are a family friend who has taken on the task of writing the obituary for the local paper or a school alumni magazine. What would you write about yourself? Not your whole life story, but the things you did and didn't do with the years that you had at your disposal. (You might actually write the obituary—it's a revealing exercise—but if you don't want to do that, at least pause for a few moments and jot down notes on a scrap of paper. You know the stuff: date of birth, parents and siblings, education, positions, honors, hobbies, and then some last sentence, "At the time of death he [she] was . . . ." (Was what? Was groping toward a new beginning, was stuck, was miles from home with the darkness falling, was running scared, was done with trying to meet the expectations of others at last . . . was what?)

Since endings are dyings in one sense, the obituary is an appropriate statement on your past. As you stand here in the emptiness of the neutral zone, what do you think and feel about that past? What was unlived in that past—what dreams, what convictions, what talents, what ideas, what qualities in you went unrealized? You are at a turning point now. The next phase of your life is taking shape. This is an opportunity to do something different with your life, something that expresses you in some significant way. This is a chance to begin a new chapter.

6. *Take a few days to go on your own version of a passage journey.* Several times I have said that it is impossible to reinstate the old rites of passage. Like trans-

plants from an alien organism, they seldom "take" in a modern setting. They are shaped by and for a sensibility that we have lost, and they depend on a lifetime of exposure to ceremonies and mental disciplines. Yet that does not mean that there is no way to mark or to dramatize your own inner changes. As I noted, you probably unwittingly do that already in taking time out to be alone at transition times in your life. What I am suggesting here is not that you learn about rituals and patch one together for yourself—only that you go further in the natural tendency to withdraw for a time during the neutral-zone phase of transition. What I am suggesting is that you spend a few days alone, during which you reflect consciously on the transition process in your own life just now.

The place should be an unfamiliar one and free of the ordinary influences from your daily situation, as was the initiate's journey of old. The simpler and quieter the setting, the more chance you will have to attend to your inner business. Your food should be simple, and your meals should be small. Leave at home the wonderful novel you've been meaning to read, and don't distract yourself with other entertainment. Take along a notebook to jot in, but don't feel that you have to write anything substantial while you are there.

This retreat is a journey into emptiness and a time to cultivate receptivity. The more you leave behind, the more room you have to find something new. Do what you do attentively, rather than distractedly while you wait for the *real* experience to come along. Making tea and putting on your shoes and seeing a bird on the bush outside the window are the real experience. Every detail is worth noticing—each is a note in the great symphony, peep-toot-and-boom.

If it appeals to you, keep a vigil during one of your nights—that is, stay awake all night with no activity more demanding then keeping a fire going or getting something to drink occasionally. Since the idea is to stay awake, you'll want to sit up rather than lie down, and it will help to get up and walk around from time to time.

There are no secrets to taking a neutral-zone retreat, no great topics that you are supposed to meditate on. You are simply living for a little while in a setting that corresponds to your position in life. You've removed the old reality-glasses and are looking at the world anew. For this special time take note of your hunches and the coincidences that happen and the crazy ideas that occur to you and the dreams that you remember for those first few seconds in the morning. If you think of little symbolic actions you could perform in this place, go ahead and do them. One person scratches out a design with a stick in the dust and then sits in the middle; another writes out a description of all that she has been trying to do in the last year and then burns it; another talks to the full moon; and still another carves strange spirals on the handle of a new-found walking stick. You can figure out what things mean later. For now, enter as fully as you can into whatever process is taking place.

A word of caution, though. The advice to participate in such a process is not an excuse to do foolhardy things. The midnight hike through the woods is likely to leave you with a whopping case of poison oak or ivy. The lonely swim in the surf might cost you your life. This is a time for doing things that you wouldn't normally do, but it is not a time to hurt yourself.

Mostly it is a time to do whatever you do as though it were an element in an elaborate and ancient ritual and to do it with your total attention. For once in your life, you don't have to produce any results or accomplish anything. If you are happy, be happy. If you are bored, be bored. If you are lonely or sad, be lonely or sad. There is not some better reaction you could be having to the experience.

Whatever you are feeling is *you,* and you're there to be alone with that very person.

Since a life transition is a kind of buried rite of passage to begin with, a person's life will take on, willy-nilly, symbolic overtones at such times. The value of reflecting on the symbolism and making up little private rituals is not for the sake of ceremony but simply to become more aware of the shape of the natural transition process. Dying, the neutral zone, and rebirth are not ideas that we bring to life; they are phenomena that we find in life. The only trick is to see them—by looking beyond the reflected light of the familiar surface of things and seeing what is really there, working in the depths.

The neutral zone—the time between the old life and the new—is a particularly rich time for such insight. As I describe the transition process, I am conscious of simplifying it for purposes of readier identification. I have been saying, for example, that the order of transition is ending, then neutral zone, then new beginning. In fact things do not stay lined up in their proper order. What I have been calling the in-between place of neutrality may actually precede any visible ending. Or it may come after a supposed beginning.

You see the former case when someone "goes dead" at work or around the home. There has been no ending, no disengagement. The old job or the old relationship is intact. But the person is *not there.* He or she has become unplugged emotionally. Sometimes this happens because a decision has been made inwardly to end the situation. Emotionally, an ending has already taken place, although the outer circumstances remain unchanged. Or it may happen because of a great disappointment—the failure to get an expected promotion, for example. Again, a subtle inner ending takes place, although everything goes on as before on the outside. In such cases the neutral zone overlaps with the old life, and the person moves like a sleepwalker through a role that was once identified with.

It often happens, however, that the external ending and the new beginning stand side by side with no room for a neutral space between them. The person moves from one town to another and the new life begins. Or from one job to another with no time off between them. Or a relationship begins, and there is no real ending to being alone. In such cases one is likely to be well into the new beginning before waking up to the fact that it is all strange and unreal. We say then that we "aren't used to the new situation yet," and it is true that things will seem less strange when the setting and the cues are more familiar. But it is also true that the strangeness comes from a belated encounter with the neutral zone.

Whether it overlaps with the old situation because inwardly some ending has already taken place, or whether it overlaps with the new situation because an inner new beginning has not yet been made, the neutral zone is a time of inner reorientation. It is the phase of the transition process that the modern world pays least attention to. Treating ourselves like appliances that can be unplugged and plugged in again at will or cars that stop and start with the twist of a key, we have forgotten the importance of fallow time and winter and rests in music. We have abandoned a whole system of dealing with the neutral zone through ritual, and we have tried to deal with personal change as though it were a matter of some kind of readjustment.

In so doing, we have lost any way of making sense out of the lostness and the confusion that we encounter when we have gone through disengagement or disenchantment or disidentification. We are like Alice at the bottom of the rabbit hole, muttering,

"It'll be no use their putting their heads down and saying, 'Come up again, dear!' I shall only look up and say Who am I, then? Tell me that first, and then, if I like being that person, I'll come up: if not, I'll stay down here till I'm somebody else—but, oh dear!" cried Alice, with a sudden burst of tears. "I do wish they would put their heads down! I am so very tired of being all alone here!"[9]

It *is* lonely down there—except that there are more people down there than you are likely to realize.

As Arnold Toynbee pointed out, it is into some rabbit hole or cave or forest wilderness that creative individuals have always withdrawn on the eve of their rebirth. "The pattern of withdrawal and return," he called it, and he traced it out in the lives of St. Paul, St. Benedict, Gregory the Great, the Buddha, Muhammad, Machiavelli, and Dante.[10]

It is reassuring to find great figures groping through the darkness of the neutral zone, although we may still doubt that we will come across any burning bushes or that a whole lifetime under a bo tree would produce enlightenment. Our own lives may be drawn with a smaller brush and our moments of discovery may be less grand—but the pattern is the same and it is even there in our own pasts, if we will look.

6

MAKING A BEGINNING

He has half the deed done, who has
made a beginning.

HORACE
Epistles[1]

In this book, as in the transition process, we come to
beginnings only at the end. It is when the endings and the
time of fallow neutrality are finished that we can launch
ourselves out anew, changed and renewed by the destruction of the old life-phase and the journey through the
nowhere.

This simple truth goes against the grain of our
mechanistic culture. We live in a context where things
start with a switch or a key. If things don't start properly,
there are procedures to follow in order to discover what is
wrong. For something is surely wrong—mechanisms are
made to start when we want them to.

These assumptions even influence the way in which
we deal with that primal beginning, childbirth. Although
there is evidence that attitudes are changing, birth has
usually been regarded in this country as a surgical procedure, and pregnancy as a form of disability. The baby was
taken and the mother *put to sleep* while the technicians
did their work. The implications of these attitudes are
far-reaching, for as a society views birth, so it will view
rebirth. Just as our primal beginning is mechanized, so
are all subsequent beginnings through our lifetime; they are
viewed as occasions for getting things started again after
they have stopped. Without fully realizing it, we tend to
imagine that somewhere there are psychological obstetri-
cians who know how to get us out, whack us on the back,
and get us functioning again. Even as you start reading
this chapter on the new beginning, you may well be wait-

ing for the procedure that must surely be here somewhere—the checklist that you're supposed to run through when life has stalled and refuses to start up again properly.

I appreciate the difficulty, for I've struggled with it myself ever since I ended my career as a college teacher. How do I know (I keep wondering) when the ending is complete and when I've been in the neutral zone long enough? How do I know which path before me represents a genuine beginning, or which footprints represent a real path, or even which marks in the dust are real footprints? It's all very well to talk about new phases of life, but they're not different colors, the way the states were on our grammar school maps. There are times when I long for some simple way out, some procedure to follow rather than a process to understand.

But my life, and yours, goes forward regardless, and even as we look in vain for ways to get the machinery going again, we are doing unwittingly much of what we need to do to be renewed and changed. We forget how indirect and unimpressive beginnings really are, and we imagine instead some clear and conscious steps that we ought to be taking. English novelist John Galsworthy was surely right when he wrote, "The beginnings . . . of all human undertakings are untidy."[2]

Think back to the important beginnings in your own past. You bumped into an old friend that you hadn't seen for years, and he told you about a job at his company that opened up just that morning. You met your spouse-to-be at a party that you really hadn't wanted to go to and that you almost skipped. You learned to play the guitar while you were getting over the measles, and you learned French because the Spanish class met at 8:00 A.M. and you hated to get up early. You happened to pick up a book that totally changed your life because it was the only one lying on your friend's coffee table—and later you were astonished to find that you had once tried to read it before, but had found it dull and confusing.

The lesson in all such experiences is that when we are ready to make a beginning, we will shortly find an opportunity. The transition process involves an inner realignment and a renewal of energy, both of which depend on immersion in the chaos of the neutral zone. It is as though the form that we call "my life" had to return occasionally to pure energy in order to take a new shape and gain new momentum. This is why in archaic cultures the myths of the creation of the world are recited over a sick person. As the scholar Mircea Eliade has written:

> *By making the patient symbolically . . .*
> *contemporary with the Creation, he lived*
> *again in the initial plenitude of being. One*
> *does not* repair *a worn-out organism, it must*
> *be* re-made; *the patient needs to be born*
> *again; he needs, as it were, to recover the*
> *whole energy and potency that a being has at*
> *the moment of its birth.*[3]

No wonder it makes such a difference how a culture views birth, and no wonder we long for some way of avoiding the pain of rebirth.

Therefore much as we long for external signs that point the way to the future, we must settle for inner signals that alert us to the proximity of new beginnings. The most important of these signals begins as a faint intimation of something different, a new theme in the music, a strange fragrance on the breeze. Because the signal is subtle, it is hard to perceive when other stimuli are strong—which is why we naturally, if unconsciously, seek emptiness and quietness in times of life-transition.

This first hint may take the form of either an inner idea or of an external opportunity, but its hallmark is not a logical sign of validity but a resonance that it sets up in us.

With many of the people in transition that I've worked with, this first hint came in the form of an "idea" or an "impression" or an "image." There is no single word for the experience, but it involves imagining some scene or activity and feeling attracted to it. You may well be doing that already and not realizing it, for the experience is right at the lower edge of consciousness—something like a half-formed daydream. One of the women in the transition class had been imagining herself working with disturbed children for several years without ever realizing that this was, in fact, something that she wanted to do. One of the men in the class had a whole business venture planned out in fantasy, again without ever having acknowledged to himself that it represented a potential next step in his life.

Sometimes the hint comes in the form of a comment that somebody drops and that you find yourself remembering. "You depend so much on research," a friend told an aspiring writer in the transition class, "but the things I like best in your writing come from your own experience." That was one of those reactions that one might easily forget, but this woman could not forget it: "It nagged away at me," she said, "as though it were the answer to all my confusion—although it took me a year to see what the answer really meant."

In other cases, the hint comes in the form of a dream—which reminds us how often traditional cultures taught their people to watch their dreams for signs of guidance. One member of the transition class had long been playing with the idea of doing something more serious with her skill as a weaver. "Place mats at Christmas are nice, but I have the feeling that that's not enough," she said. Then she dreamed that she went home and entered the front door, only to find a strange corridor stretching out to the left where, in fact, there was only a blank wall. She went down the corridor, then down some stairs, and finally found herself in a small underground bedroom that apparently belonged to a small girl. She was astonished that she hadn't known about this room in her house before, but something about it was very appealing to her and she wondered who lived in it. "I wish it had been a studio or an art gallery," she said as we talked about dreams and guidance. It was only much later, when other signs had pointed her in that direction, that she recognized that her childhood fantasy-world was what she wanted to depict in tapestried image—and thus she began a career as a serious and successful artist.

This woman, like most of us, was looking too literally at the signs her life was providing her. She wanted to be an artist and she expected a signal, *yea* or *nay*. She wanted an answer, and so she almost overlooked the fact that she was being given a path to follow. It was almost as though her dream had said, "Don't *be* something, *do* something." It was only when she stopped trying to be the artist that she began to explore the strange corridor in her life that she had never noticed before and found in the half-buried world of the little girl a way of looking at the world that unlocked her natural talent and aligned her with her future.

Genuine beginnings depend upon this kind of inner realignment rather than on external shifts, for when we are aligned with deep longings (the real wantings discussed in Chapter 5), we become powerfully motivated. Again and again, I have watched with amazement as people who are motivated in this way overcome what I would have taken to be insuperable obstacles to reach their goals. A woman of forty, for example, just divorced, with three children, one of them seriously handicapped.

With no college education, she had every reason to settle for the immediate solution of office work at a low salary. But she wanted to be a college teacher! "That will take *years*," everyone warned her. But one step at a time, she followed a path that led her through college, graduate school, and a frustrating period of temporary jobs, and finally to the teaching job she had dreamed of.

Or the doctor in his forties who had always wanted to be a percussionist in an orchestra. As a college student he had been diverted by family pressure from following such an "impractical" dream, but now at fifty he had lived out their plan for him and had accumulated a modest fortune in real estate. He was in a comfortable rut, doing things mechanically and wondering at the emptiness of his life. A friend's daughter went to a music school one summer and played in the symphony there, and he found himself imagining that he was doing the same thing. The next year he arranged to take a month off and he returned to school. The impact was astounding. By the time he returned, his mind was made up. The shift wasn't easy, however, for his whole life had to be rebuilt economically. It meant different kinds of investments, a smaller house, a loan to pay the kids' college tuition. It also meant a complicated process of terminating patients and disengaging himself from active practice—not to mention lessons and auditions and practice. But he did it, against the advice of family and friends who said that he'd miss the affluence and the excitement. "And I do miss them," he said, the last time I talked to him, "but I've also never been happier."

I emphasize vocational changes in these examples because it is when things come down to money and time that people always say that they just can't manage to launch the new beginning they dream of. Examples of this sort are much commoner than most people realize, for until recently the image of the linear lifetime and the linear career has so dominated our outlook and defined our expectations that we have underestimated how often people do make radical new beginnings during the course of adulthood. Nor have we realized how often important accomplishments come from such turning points.

We all learned in school, for example, about Abraham Lincoln's youth—the poverty and the ambition and the sense of responsibility of a frontier boy. The history books imply that our greatest president was shaped by his childhood. But in fact that childhood produced a young adult who was not very remarkable—a man who did this and that, and had a difficult marriage, a not very successful term in Congress, and terrible bouts of melancholy. It was not from boyhood but from a profound transition in his thirties that this man stepped forth into history. It was only then that he discovered where he was going and what he could really do. Out of a dark time in his own inner neutral zone, Lincoln found the seeds of his future; and from there he began a rapid rise to prominence that no one could have predicted for him only a few years earlier.

Gandhi, Eleanor Roosevelt, Mother Teresa of Calcutta, Walt Whitman—the names of famous people who began anew in the midst of adult life-transitions are plentiful. Some discovered what they really wanted and then made their changes, while others found life taking the lead and only subsequently discovered in unchosen transitions the opportunities to do what they seem to have been destined to do.

But there is a danger in citing too many of these examples, for it suggests that only great people or unusually talented ones can follow the path of self-renewal through transition; it suggests that only special people can make new beginnings during the adult years. And since such people represent such clear successes, it is easy to imagine that the doubts and confusions that we feel when we are trying to make a new beginning are signs of bad timing, or lack of potential, or a wrong direction.

The truth is otherwise, and anyone who is trying to launch a new beginning needs to understand that fact. New beginnings are accessible to everyone, and everyone has trouble with them. Much as we may wish to make a new beginning, some part of us resists doing so as though we were making the first step toward disaster. Everyone has a slightly different version of these anxieties and confusions, but in one way or another they all arise from the fear that real change destroys the old ways in which we established our security. To act on the basis of what we really want is to say, "I, a unique person, exist." It is to assert that we are on our own in a much deeper sense than we ever imagined when we were originally setting up shop as adults. That process involved only independence; this involves autonomy.

The great people point the way for us, though too often they cover up the evidence of their confusion. Eleanor Roosevelt looked back on her own painful life-transition at thirty-five and wrote, "Somewhere along the line of development we discover what we really are, and then we make our real decision for which we are responsible. Make that decision primarily for yourself because you can never really live anyone else's life, not even your own child's."[4] What she did not say was that her discovery was won after a time of disenchantment and disorientation that almost killed her. She had discovered that her husband was having an affair with one of her most trusted friends. It was out of the shattered dream of domestic safety that she emerged, struggling against her own shyness and self-doubt, to become an important public figure in her own right.

To make a successful new beginning, it is important to do more than simply persevere. It is important to understand what it is within us that undermines our resolve and casts doubt on our plans. One member of the transition class was close to the truth when he said, "There's a tough old immigrant inside me who is scared to death of anything new and who believes that the only way to survive is to do everything the old, slow, safe way." This man was a scientist whose parents were, in fact, immigrants who had lived out their lives in the narrow corridors of a city ghetto. While he himself had made many external changes, he still lived by the safety code that they had taught him in childhood. No chances—take no chances. His life was a spider web of precautions, and he picked up every threat to his life-system through subtle vibrations along the strands.

Then came his transition. In this case it was marital difficulty—his wife began to feel like a fly in the web—but it might well have been related to work or health or finances. Being reasonable, this man could see the changes that he had to make. He could even feel the excitement of a new and less restrictive relationship with his wife. "In holding her less tightly, I'd free myself too," he said. "The guard is a prisoner too, you know."

But each step forward set off an inner warning system, and he would retreat in confusion to the old ways of being. One day he was ready to launch a new life, and the next he was bitterly suspicious about the motives of others and his own promptings. "What am I trying to prove?" he would ask belligerently. "My life's not so bad as it is!" and then he would go through a time of resisting change and undermining all temptations to go for what he really deeply wanted at that point in his life—more freedom, more energy, and new goals.

This particular man finally decided to begin psychotherapy, for the inner resistance to transition was too great for him to deal with on his own. For many people, however, this is not so. Identifying their inner resistance and understanding the symptoms of its activity may be enough.[5] They may find that this inner reactionary (as one woman called it) is stirring up trouble in a relationship. They may find themselves being unwittingly belligerent or provocative, almost as though they were trying to start a fight so that they had an excuse to say, "There, that proves it. He [she] won't let me change." Or they may find themselves plunging unexpectedly into a depression at the prospect of a new beginning—and find on closer examination that the inner reactionary is muttering, "All right, if you won't do what I say, I'll bring this whole show to a standstill." Or they may find themselves getting confused and forgetting what it is they want, as if the inner reactionary were saying, "So you won't pay any attention to my warnings, huh? OK, then, I'll fog up your brain so that you won't remember where you are, and then you'll have to cancel that big trip you're planning."

It is as though each of us had some inner figure whose idea of caring for us involved only taking us into protective custody whenever we threatened in the transition process to become too autonomous. Some people find the figure activated whenever risk is involved, while others experience the inner sabotage whenever they try to come in from the cold and settle down. One person's safety involves inactivity and another's involves perpetual motion. In either case, a new beginning upsets a long-standing arrangement.

The same thing happens externally in relationships, and beginnings often bring conflict and even a sense of betrayal. The person's imminent change sets off danger signals in the other, for it rightly suggests that the old tacit agreements on which the relationship was based will have to be renegotiated. "You be this way and I'll be that way" doesn't work any more, because now *I* want to be that way and you . . . well, you will have to do some changing too. This is something that can only be dealt with openly and honestly, for indirection or denial only increase the other's resistance.

It is important to distinguish between a real new beginning in someone's life and a simple defensive reaction to an ending. Each may exert strain on a relationship, but the new beginning must be honored, while the defensive reaction is simply a new way of perpetuating the old situation and needs to be considered as such.

On the second or third night of the transition class, for example, one of the men arrived in a state of bitterness and frustration. His forty-year marriage was on the rocks, he said, and it was all because his wife could not adjust to the new situation resulting from his recent retirement. He began to think that she just wanted him for a paycheck, he said with heavy sighs, and now that he was there as a person, she didn't really care for him.

We were well into a state of commiseration when someone thought to ask him exactly what had happened to show him this side of his wife. It turned out that he had reorganized the kitchen for her, and she had kicked him out of the house. A very precise and orderly man who had been used to supervising others, he discovered in the empty first days of his new leisure a fresh field for his talents—the kitchen cupboards. His wife had come home from a trip to the city to find everything in the kitchen in some new place, with a neat label on each shelf and a list on the back of each cupboard door. "Look what I got for trying to help her," he said bitterly.

This man honestly believed that his actions were part of the transition process. ("I never *used* to help around the house before," he said.) He claimed that his wife couldn't stand for him to change. In fact, however, it was *he* who couldn't stand to change—who couldn't go through the whole three-phase transition process to a new beginning. Instead, he was just perpetuating his old style and activity in a new way. He was avoiding an ending and calling the result a new beginning.

Unfortunately, there is no psychological litmus paper we can use to test ourselves at such times. Often it is difficult to be sure whether some path leads forward or back, and it may be necessary to follow it for a little way to be sure. But there are two signs that are worth looking for before you start. The first is the reaction of people who know you well: not whether they approve or disapprove, but whether they see what you propose to do as something new or simply a replay of some old pattern. The second indication comes from the transition process: Have you really moved through endings into the neutral zone and found there the beginning you now want to follow, or is this "beginning" a way of avoiding an ending or aborting the neutral-zone experience?

Genuine beginnings begin within us, even when they are brought to our attention by external opportunities. It is out of the formlessness of the neutral zone that new form emerges and out of the barrenness of the fallow time that new life springs. We can support and even enhance the process, but we cannot produce the results. Once those results begin to take shape, however, there are several things that can be done.

The first is, very simply, to stop getting ready and to act. Getting ready can turn out to be an endless task, and one of the forms that inner resistance often takes is the attempt to make just a few more (and then more, and again more) preparations. It is true, of course, that timing is important in any new undertaking. (You may remember trying again and again to lose weight or stop smoking or start jogging—and then one day you discover that it seems to happen almost by itself.) Yes, until you are really ready, you probably won't make a real beginning. But that does not mean that your odds are improved by trying to "get ready." When the time comes, stop getting ready to do it—and do it!

The second thing you can do is to begin to identify yourself with the final result of the new beginning. What is it going to feel like when you've actually done whatever it is that you are setting out to do? All right, then, say it's done. There, you did it. You are the person who does that sort of thing. People look at you now as the-one-who-did-it, and seeing yourself through their eyes, you realize what self-confidence is: experiencing yourself as one who can do things like that. You can see that it is your way of looking at other people that endows them with that special power or ability to do things that you used to think you lacked. Their specialness and difference from you was a mantle that you laid over their shoulders, and you can take it back now and wear it yourself.

I go through this routine myself at the beginning of every new project. (You'd think I'd learn and not keep making the same old self-defeating mistakes over and over, but I don't ever seem to get it, once and for all.) Let's say that it is a conference that I'm putting together, and I am calling people to ask them to be keynote speakers. The first few calls are agonizing. Somehow I feel as though I am *nobody* talking to *somebody*. Who am I to ask them? I probably sound like someone saying, "I know that you probably won't want to do this dreary, foolish thing that I am about to suggest, but just in case you are feeling extra charitable today, would you consider talking at my insignificant, dull conference?"

Then I get a grip on myself and recall what it feels like after a couple of speakers have accepted. I imagine that the conference is almost staffed and that the cast of presenters is really impressive. I'm really offering my next caller an unusual opportunity to take part in something exciting and valuable. "Hello," I say, and my voice sounds different now, even to me. "This is Bill Bridges." (I don't need to tell you that I'm the one who puts on those wonderful conferences, do I?) "I'd like to talk to you about a conference I'm setting up." (You lucky devil!)

Such strategies have only a temporary effect, and they do no good if the undertaking in question is not something that has roots deep in your own wanting. And even when it does, there will be times of losing momentum, times when your inner reactionary says, "What difference will it make anyway? Wouldn't you rather be (a) taking a nap, (b) lying on the beach, (c) eating peanut butter cookies, or (d) waiting for someone else to do the project?" The answers are, respectively, yes, yes, yes, and yes. But you also know by now something about your own resistances to transition and how important it is to go on with the transition process in spite of them.

This is where the third thing to do is important: Take things step by step and resist the siren song that tells of some other route where everything is exciting and meaningful. In making any beginning, you can become so invested in the results that whatever you have to do to reach them looks very insignificant. Trudging from appointment to appointment, licking stamps, adding columns of figures, making reminder phone calls, and explaining your idea for the hundredth time—these are the trivia from which vital new ventures finally emerge. But by comparison with the goal, they seem hopelessly dull.

In any important new beginning, a preoccupation with results can be very damaging. There was a vocational counselor in the transition class who had recently moved to our area and was looking for a new job. He had given himself three months to find it, but before a month was out he reported that he wasn't making it. Every interview that did not produce a job became a *failure* and everything he said had been, he suspected, a *mistake*.

It was only when he shifted his attention from the intended goal to the process of investigation that he lost this sense of discouragement—and, not coincidentally I think, found a job quickly. Instead of seeing the interviews as shots at a target (damn, missed again!) he saw them as elements in a comprehensive process. Each interview taught him something or created a new contact or deepened his understanding of himself. He saw himself as searching and learning, rather than as not finding what he was after. And in the process, he learned the fourth important thing to remember in making a beginning, which is to diffuse your purpose and transfer it from the goal to the process of reaching the goal.

This advice is not simply a way of checking your disappointment when your progress is slow. It also represents the inner side of the transition process—which is a process, after all, and not a three-positioned switch. Even though the external "new beginning" may happen very quickly once it becomes evident, the internal identification and engagement occur more slowly. Many of the old passage rituals recognized this fact by bringing the renewed person back from the neutral zone in several steps and over a period of some time—a few days or weeks being spent in a couple of "halfway houses" along the way back to the village.

Like so much else about the transition process, we have lost the social mores that once structured beginnings. But we can nevertheless draw on that lore to act wisely and considerately in our own behalf and our treatment of others. It is unrealistic to expect someone to make a beginning like a sprinter coming out of the starting blocks. Even when the outer situation is complete—you're on the new job, you're finally married, you're in the new house—the inner beginnings are still going on. It is a time to be gentle with yourself or with the other person, a time for the little supports and indulgences that make things easier.

Not everything vanishes in the ending process, of

course, and some people find it very important to experience the continuities in their lives when so much else is changing. I am typing these words right now on our dining room table, for example, a table that my parents bought before I was born, a table that I ate all my childhood meals on, a table that represents to me the whole New England world that is my background. And now, living in California, raising my children differently from the way I was raised, directing my life toward goals that are very different from those with which I started, I find real pleasure in the fact that this important new beginning of mine is being written on something that is old and dear to me.

It is, after all, a new chapter of *my* life that is beginning. I haven't become somebody else. The beginning isn't happening to some "him" that rose up new and complete. The transition process is really a loop in the life-journey, a going out and away from the main flow for a time and then a coming around and back. The neutral zone is meant to be only a temporary state. It is, as they say, a great place to visit, but you wouldn't want to live there. When the neutral zone has done its work, you come back.

Socially, this means that the isolated person returns from the disengaged state and the wilderness to set about translating insight and idea into action and form. This return may take the form of new commitments at home and at work: the person is really *there* again after a time of being "somewhere else." The same return may take the person into new relationships or projects. But either way, the old connections that were broken with the earlier disengagement are now replaced.

Psychologically, the process of return brings us back to ourselves and involves a reintegration of the new identity and elements of the old one. This connection is necessary if one is to be grounded and not "up in the clouds." This aspect of the beginning is as natural as the *dis*integration was back in the termination phase. Inwardly and outwardly, one *comes home.* As a wonderful Zen saying expresses it, "After enlightenment, the laundry."

Endings and beginnings, with emptiness and germination in between. That is the shape of the transition periods in our lives, and these times come far more frequently in adulthood and cut far more deeply into it than most of us imagined that they would. But the same process is also going on continuously in our lives. As humankind once knew and celebrated, the same rhythm puts us to sleep at night and wakes us in the morning after a dark time full of half-remembered and enigmatic clues. It takes us through the turning year, around to an ending which opens out on to a new beginning. And so it is with our lives—a dozen little endings, hardly noticed in the day-to-day rush, plunge us into little wildernesses; a dozen little beginnings, taking shape in confusion and emerging unexpectedly into clear form. ("Where did *that* idea come from?" "When did you decide that?")

Endings and beginnings, with emptiness and germination in between. That basic shape is so essential to growth that we must learn to recognize it in our lives. Those societies that were most knowledgeable about it and designed rituals to facilitate it had, however, little faith in descriptions. Words failed to portray the experience and to reach deep enough in the mind to have a lasting effect. For that reason, these societies couched their most important insights in the form of myths. So it was with Oedipus and the riddle of the sphinx, and so it was with the story of Odysseus and the homeward journey. To summarize the basic transition process, we turn in conclusion to another myth: the story of Amor and Psyche.

EPILOGUE

Not in his goals but in his
transitions man is great.

RALPH WALDO EMERSON[1]

Once upon a time—which is to say, right now and from
the beginning and till the end—there was a very lovely
young woman. She was, in fact, the loveliest woman in
the whole kingdom, but although this was universally
admitted, no one courted her. Others married and began
families, but Psyche (for that was her name) seemed too
perfect for any ordinary mortal.[2]

Psyche's parents finally sent to the great oracle at Delphi for an answer, and the answer came back. But when
they heard it, they wept, for the oracle said that Psyche
must die. Dressed in funeral clothes, Psyche was to be
taken to a wild and desolate crag in the mountains on the
far side of the kingdom. There she was to be abandoned.

*In stories one does not ask why, for everything goes
according to a plan that is patterned on life itself. What
the oracle is saying is simply that no new time of life is
possible without the death of the old lifetime. To gain,
you must first give up.*

So they dressed Psyche in funeral clothes and con-
ducted her death-rites and left her on the cold and windy
mountaintop. As she lay there, numb with fear and sunk
in despair, Amor, the god of passionate love, came to her
side. Gazing on her perfection, he himself fell in love with
her. Quickly he flew off to get the West Wind, his helper,
and to ask him to carry Psyche down into the hidden valley
beneath the mountaintops where Amor had a dark palace.

Thus it was that when she awoke, Psyche found herself in a mysteriously beautiful castle. Everything she
could possibly need was there—food and drink, lovely
clothing, perfumed baths, everything but companionship.

But then when darkness fell, she found that she had that too, for Amor came to her in the darkness and slept with her. Night after night he did this. Sometimes they talked all night, sometimes they made love, and sometimes they dined and fell asleep at once. Psyche could not have asked for more. She was happy at last.

As always happens, an ending clears the ground for a new beginning. In this case, the person did little—everything just happened. Some transitions are like that. They just happen. But when they happen this way, there is something missing. The outer situation has taken shape, but the inner state remains unchanged. The old outlook, the old self-image, the old value system remain intact. Outwardly the change is complete, but the real transition process has hardly begun.

In time Psyche began to feel a strange incompleteness about her life. Everything was perfect, but she missed her old friends and her family. This hidden palace was indeed beautiful, but it was also unreal—outside the real world, outside time, outside human connections. She talked of this to her secret lover. She told him that she wished to see her family again. Could her sisters come and visit her, perhaps?

Amor at first refused, but she longed so for contact with her family that he at last relented. They must come, he said, when he was away, and they must be gone before his return. She was delighted and promised to do as he said.

The sisters came, carried by the same West Wind that brought Psyche originally to this paradise. They were amazed—and jealous. Who was this secret lover, they asked? Psyche did not know, of course, but she made up stories. (She had never, in fact, seen him since he only came in the darkness and never showed her his face.) Psyche hid her ignorance as well as she could, but it was not long before her answers began contradicting each

other. "You don't even know what he looks like!" cried the
sisters. "Why, he is probably a great beast that uses the
darkness to hide his awful ugliness! You have been a fool.
You have a wicked and loathsome animal for a lover."

When they left, Psyche was desperate with confusion.
He seemed like a gentle, loving person. But it was true
that he never let her see him. Her sisters' suspicions filled
her head, and she vowed to find out the truth for herself.
Late that night after he had fallen asleep, she crept out
and found a candle and a knife. She would steal a look at
him, and if he were the terrible creature her sisters said he
must be, she would stab him.

She lit the candle in the hall, and tiptoed up to the bed
where he slept. Raising the candle in one hand and the
knife in the other, she leaned over his bed. There he lay,
the handsomest of gods! Amor, her lover. In her excitement, her hand trembled and hot wax fell onto the sleeping god's shoulder. He woke. In a moment he saw what
she had done, and he told her that, having broken the rule
of darkness, she would never henceforth see him again.
Suddenly he was gone, and Psyche was alone, stunned by
what she had done and its effect.

*In the everyday world of fact, agreements are meant
to be kept, but in the world of myth everything happens
for a reason and points toward some further end. Losses
happen because it is time to let go of that way of being
connected. Psyche had lived in the darkness for long
enough, and it was now time to see. Yet the change was a
violation of the old rules, and it destroyed the old situation. It was time for her to change—to grow and deepen,
to take responsibility for who and where she was. It was
time for the inner changes to catch up with the outer
ones.*

So Psyche left the palace where she had been so
happy, and began a lonely journey in search of her lost
lover. In her grief, she called upon the gods for help, and

one of them, the great Aphrodite, answered. "You seek my son," she said, for she was the mother of Amor, "but I think that you are not strong enough to do what must be done." Psyche said that that was not so; she would do anything.

"Very well. You must complete four difficult tasks," said Aphrodite. "First, you must sort out this roomful of seeds—putting each type of seed in a separate pile—in a single night." She threw open a door, and there Psyche saw a large room piled high with all kinds of seeds jumbled together in one immense heap. She gasped at the impossibility of the task, but Aphrodite continued without a pause. "Second, you must go to the field where the fire-breathing rams with the golden fleece live—and bring me back some of that fleece." Psyche was stunned, for those rams killed anyone who entered their field. "And third," Aphrodite said before Psyche had time to recover, "You must bring me back a goblet of water from the great river—the River Styx—that plunges off the inaccessible cliffs and into the underworld." She looked at Psyche, amused at the hopeless look on the mortal's face.

"And finally," she said, "you must go down into hell itself and ask Persephone for a little box of her magic ointment that enhances one's beauty miraculously. Get it and bring it back to me." And having said that, Aphrodite vanished.

Psyche was stunned. Sadly, she opened the door and gazed on her first task. The pile of seeds was higher than her head, and it covered the floor of a good-sized room. She bent over and picked up a handful of seeds. Little ones, big ones, dark ones, light ones—no one could possibly bring order to this confusion in a year of sorting, and she had one night! The enormity of her task overcame her, and she sank down weeping at the edge of the pile. Feebly, she picked over a handful or two, but she was weary and depressed, and soon she fell asleep.

*The first time her life had changed, Psyche was quite
passive—it all just happened to her. Now, however, she
was ready to act—but the tasks! They were impossible
ones! She tried to do them, but then she had to give up.
And when she did, she discovered that . . .*

As she slept, a vast army of ants came into the room.
On the command of their leaders, they began the sorting.
All night they swarmed over the huge pile, and gradually it
melted away until in its place were a dozen smaller piles
of wheat and rye and beans and mustard seeds. At sunrise
Aphrodite suddenly threw open the door and woke the
sleeping Psyche. Both of them gasped in amazement to
see the sorting done. Psyche said nothing, and Aphrodite
said only, "You have three more tasks."

With the golden fleece and the water from the Styx,
similar things happened. Just as she was about to give up
hope of getting the fleece, the reeds that grew by the river
whispered to her that if she would wait until sunset when
the rams retreat to their night's rest, she could creep up to
the edge of the field and find bits of the fleecy treasure on
the bushes. And just as she was about to abandon hope of
getting a goblet of Styx water, a great eagle flew down
from the heaven and took the vessel from her hands and
filled it from the torrent far above her head. Aphrodite was
startled each time by Psyche's success, but she only said,
"We'll see how you do with the journey to the underworld."

*What are the ants and reeds and the eagle? Why does
something appear to help Psyche each time she has
given up hope? The "helpful creature" is a common element in folklore and dreams, and it corresponds to some
instinctive and subrational level of insight and energy.
The tasks of transition are not, it seems, of the sort that
one can consciously set out to accomplish. Yet neither
are they taken care of in the automatic fashion of
Psyche's original and outer transition on the mountain-*

156

top. Now she must struggle and even exhaust herself before help arrives—almost as though it is only when one is at the end of one's resources that new and hitherto unsuspected powers appear.

But how is she to get to the underworld, survive the dangers of that region, and come back with the treasure? As she is on the verge of giving up, a tower near which she is standing begins to speak to her. He gives her instructions—bring coins to pay for her passage across the Styx, carry sweet cakes to pacify the guardian animals, and resist all requests from anyone for help. So off she goes. The coins and cakes are simple enough, but it is difficult for her to refuse the entreaties of the poor man whose donkey has dropped part of his load or the women who need assistance with their weaving or the dying man who calls pitifully after her for succor. Shutting out the sad calls from those in need, Psyche pushes onward and downward. This journey no one can make for her. She alone can make it, and in spite of temptations to abandon her errand, she succeeds. Thank goodness for the tower and its counsel!

A talking tower? Refusing to help those in need? A journey to the underworld? What is this all about? Well, most significant transitions—the sort of inner change that Psyche is dealing with—involve a time in hell. You go down before you come up. And most of these journeys must be taken alone. All our habits of caring for others (and seeing ourselves as people who would care for others) become self-defeating. We need to resist the old impulses to take care of others and instead to pay attention during this time to what we are doing and why we are doing it. We are going where we have to go if we are to do the gods' bidding. Having left behind a life that we have outgrown, we must continue the transition process to find our new life.

And the tower? Why, after all the previous help from

insects and birds and growing things, does this aid come from a human construct, an inanimate structure? It seems that in the end one needs that kind of assistance—that one's own deeper and unconscious resources are essential, but that they stop short of the goal. When one is going down the dark path into hell, some conscious plans must be made. The result is paradoxical—as was my urging you to trust your own inner process, and then my advice on what to do. So be it. The fact is that both are essential. And that in the dark times, one may have little but that dimly remembered advice to go on.

It would be nice to say that Amor was waiting when Psyche reappeared, but he was not. In fact, things took an apparently bad turn at this point. Back in the land of the living, Psyche looked indecisively at the box of magic ointment in her hand. She was tempted to open the box. Anything so valuable must be wonderful. Why should Aphrodite get it all? So she opened it. But the power of the content was too much for a mortal, and Psyche was overcome and collapsed.

Everything in a myth points to a purpose, and just as the earlier impulse to peek at her secret lover led to her quest and to a new level of awareness, so this peek opens up immense power. That is always how it is in the wilderness of the neutral zone: One encounters there forms of energy and insight that are life-transforming, but also just barely supportable. That is one reason why the old rituals were so important, for like the tower they gave direction and reassurance. That is why the sort of understanding that this book provides is so important, for without it one is caught in fearful places that make no sense. So Psyche is not just overly curious when she lifts the lid of her treasure from the underworld. She is taking the final step in becoming aware of herself and gaining power for the new status and phase of her life. For as with all people after important life transitions, she is going to be different.

No sooner had she fallen to the ground than Amor appeared and picked up the limp form and carried her up to Olympus. There, after due deliberation Psyche was made immortal. She and Amor were married, and they lived there happily ever after. . . .

. . . *Or until the next major life transition, whichever came first.*

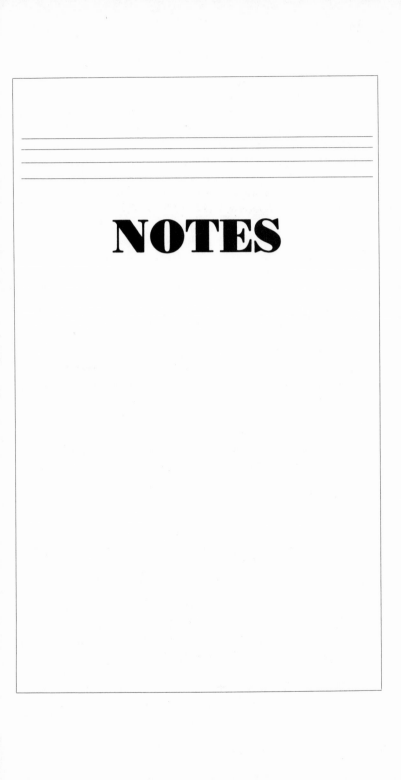

NOTES

Part I Introduction

1. Daniel J. Boorstin, *The Americans: The National Experience* (New York: Random House, 1965), pp. 92–93. The whole of Part 2, entitled "The Transients," is an interesting historical background to the present study.
2. Quoted in G. W. Pierson, *Tocqueville and Beaumont in America* (New York: Oxford University Press, 1938), p. 119.
3. *The Complete Poetical Works of Henry Wadsworth Longfellow* (Boston: Houghton Mifflin, 1893), p. 296.
4. Alvin Toffler, *Future Shock* (New York: Bantam Books, 1970), p. 12.

Chapter 1

1. Lewis Carroll, *Alice's Adventures in Wonderland* (New York: Signet Books, 1960). p. 47.
2. Mircea Eliade, *Rites and Symbols of Initiation,* trans. Willard Trask (New York: Harper & Row, 1965), p. 31.
3. This rating scale was first published in the *Journal of Psychosomatic Research* 11 (1967): 213–218. It has been reprinted in many places since, including newspaper and magazine articles and a pamphlet called *Stress* published in 1974 by Blue Cross Association, Chicago.

Chapter 2

1. Erik H. Erikson, *Identity, Youth, and Crisis* (New York: W. W. Norton, 1968), pp. 128–135.
2. Daniel J. Levinson, *The Seasons of a Man's Life* (New York: Knopf, 1978), pp. 78–84.
3. *Ibid.*, pp. 84–89, and Roger Gould, *Transformations* (New York: Simon and Schuster, 1978), pp. 153–215.
4. The most convenient summary of Buhler's work is in an article by one of her coworkers, Else Frenkel-Brunswik. Entitled "Adjustment and Reorientation in the Course of the Life Span," it is printed in Bernice L. Neugarten, ed., *Middle*

162

Age and Aging (Chicago: University of Chicago Press, 1968), pp. 77–84.

5. Levinson, *Op. cit.*, p. 141.

6. For information about late-bloomers and people who maintained a high level of productivity into the later years, see John A. B. McLeish, *The Ulyssean Adult: Creativity in the Middle and Later Years* (Toronto: McGraw-Hill–Ryerson, 1976).

7. Huston Smith, *The Religions of Man* (New York: Mentor Books, 1958), p. 64.

8. C. G. Jung, *Psychological Reflections,* ed. Jolande Jacobi (New York: Harper & Row, 1953), p. 119.

9. C. G. Jung, *Modern Man in Search of a Soul* (New York: Harcourt Brace, 1933), p. 107. More systematic and recent research suggests something that—if not so metaphorical—is similar. For example, Bernice Neugarten's "Adult Personality: Toward a Psychology of the Life Cycle" (p. 140 in Neugarten, ed.; see note 4 for full citation) where she writes, "Important differences exist between men and women as they age. Men seem to become more receptive to affiliative and nurturant promptings; women more responsive toward and less guilty about aggressive and egocentric impulses."

10. McLeish, (see note 6 for full citation).

11. Quoted in A. L. Vischer, *On Growing Old*, trans. Gerald Onn (Boston: Houghton Mifflin, 1967), p. 169.

Chapter 3

1. Erik Erikson, *Identity, Youth, and Crisis* (New York: W.W. Norton, 1968), p. 136.

Part II Introduction

1. Mircea Eliade, *The Sacred and the Profane,* trans. Willard Trask (New York: Harcourt, Brace, Jovanovich, 1959), pp. 208–209.

2. For component details see Arnold van Gennep, *Rites of Pas-*

sage, trans. Monika B. Vizedom and Gabrielle L. Chaffee
(Chicago: University of Chicago Press, 1960); Mircea
Eliade, *Rites and Symbols of Initiation,* trans. Willard
Trask (New York: Harper & Row, 1965); Victor W. Turner,
The Ritual Process (Chicago: Aldine, 1969); and Paul
Radin, *Primitive Religion* (Magnolia, Mass., Peter Smith,
1957).
3. Van Gennep (see note 2 for full citation), pp. 10–11.

Chapter 4

1. T. S. Eliot, *Four Quartets* (New York: Harcourt, Brace
1943), p. 38.
2. From a Zen story adapted by Paul Reps in *Zen Flesh, Zen
Bones* (New York: Anchor Books, n.d.), p. 18.
3. The examples come from Sam D. Gill, "Disenchantment,"
Parabola (Summer, 1976): 6–13.
4. Elisabeth Kubler-Ross, *On Death and Dying* (New York:
Macmillan, 1969), pp. 38–137.
5. Mircea Eliade, *Myths, Dreams and Mysteries,* trans. Philip
Mairet (New York: Harper & Row, 1967), p. 224.

Chapter 5

1. Lao Tzu, *Tao Te Ching,* trans. D. C. Lau (Middlesex, England: Penguin Books, 1963).
2. Carlos Castaneda, *The Teachings of Don Juan* (New York:
Ballantine Books, 1968), p. 110.
3. This quotation and an extended account of Tolstoy's crisis
appear in his autobiographical work, *A Confession,* trans.
Aylmer Maude (London: Oxford University Press, 1940).
4. Mircea Eliade, *Myths, Dreams, and Mysteries,* trans. Philip
Mairet (New York: Harper & Row, 1967) p. 80.
5. Arnold van Gennep, *Rites of Passage,* trans. Monika B. Vizedom and Gabrielle L. Chaffee (Chicago: University of
Chicago Press), p. 182.

6. "Nature," *The Complete Works of Ralph Waldo Emerson,* Vol. 1 (Boston: Houghton Mifflin, 1903), p. 4.
7. George Orwell, *1984* (New York: Signet Books, 1949), p. 189.
8. This material on *wanting* was drawn from the seminars of James Bugental.
9. Lewis Carroll, *Alice's Adventures in Wonderland* (New York: Signet Books, 1960), p. 27.
10. Arnold Toynbee, *A Study of History,* abridged by D. C. Somervell (New York: Oxford University Press, 1947), pp. 217–230.

Chapter 6

1. Horace, "To Lollius," *Epistles,* Book I, 2.
2. John Galsworthy, *Over the River* (London: William Heineman, 1933), p. 4.
3. Mircea Eliade, *Myths, Dreams and Mysteries,* trans. Philip Mairet (New York: Harper & Row, 1967), p. 48.
4. Joseph P. Lash, *Eleanor and Franklin* (New York: W. W. Norton, 1971), p. 238.
5. This inner resistance is what Mary Merrill terms the person's "dark side," and I've learned what I know about its ways from her.

Epilogue

1. Ralph Waldo Emerson, *The Journals and Miscellaneous Notebooks of Ralph Waldo Emerson,* Vol. 5, ed. Merton M. Sealts, Jr. (Cambridge, Mass.: Harvard University Press, 1965), p. 38.
2. This tale, originally told by the Latin writer Apulieus, has been studied, though not from this perspective, by several modern psychologists who used it to illustrate aspects of feminine psychology. See Robert A. Johnson, *She— Understanding Feminine Psychology* (New York: Harper & Row, 1976) and Erich Neumann, *Amor and Psyche* (Princeton: Princeton University Press, 1956).

Index

Index

Index